**Praise for M**

"At a time when we are so aware ... ...nd Christianity, Lauren Winner's book on what we can learn from each other is so refreshingly welcome."
—Rabbi Harold Kushner, author of *When Bad Things Happen to Good People*

"[Winner is] a gifted writer who has much to teach us about the deep and indestructible bonds between Judaism and Christianity."
—Richard Mouw, past President, Fuller Seminary

"A compelling engaging (and at times appropriately humorous) tour of rarely exposed yet Biblically rooted spiritual disciplines."
—*Relevant Magazine*

"The strongest reason to read this book . . . is that it makes one think. I have been considering some of her statements and discussing them with friends ever since I read the book, and I've ordered copies for close friends and recommended it to just about anyone who would listen to me. Book clubs would have much to talk about after reading this, and it should have a beneficial impact on our Christian community, if we will listen."
—*The Living Church*

"*Mudhouse Sabbath* not only reminds us that Christianity is fundamentally birthed from and nurtured by the Jewish tradition but invites us to reconnect with this rich heritage. Here we are encouraged to feed our Christian faith by planting deep roots in the fertile soil of Jewish spirituality and practice."
—Peter Rollins, author of *How (Not) To Speak of God*

"Lauren Winner speaks the language of this generation. It is authentic, free and bold."
—Ben Young, author of *The Ten Commandments of Dating*

"For all of us who can't get our spiritual lives in shape by shipping out to a monastery, Lauren Winner explores simple, do-able ways of keeping company with God in the ordinary, day-to-day world of eating, working, resting, romancing, aging, earning, grieving, and celebrating. Her rich identity as a Jewish/Christian/scholar/writer informs every sentence."
—Brian McLaren, pastor and author of *A New Kind of Christian*

Photography: Jen Fariello

**LAUREN F. WINNER** is the author of numerous books, including *Girl Meets God, Mudhouse Sabbath, Still: Notes on a Mid-faith Crisis,* and *Wearing God.* She has appeared on PBS's Religion & Ethics Newsweekly and has written for the *New York Times Book Review,* the *Washington Post Book World, Publishers Weekly, Books and Culture,* and *Christianity Today.* Winner has degrees from Duke, Columbia, and Cambridge universities, and holds a PhD in history. Lauren teaches at Duke Divinity School and lives in Durham, North Carolina. Lauren travels extensively to lecture and teach.

# MUDHOUSE SABBATH

## An Invitation to a Life of Spiritual Discipline

STUDY EDITION

## Lauren F. Winner

PARACLETE PRESS

BREWSTER, MASSACHUSETTS

*Mudhouse Sabbath: An Invitation to a Life of Spiritual Discipline—Study Edition*

2015 First Printing This Edition

*Mudhouse Sabbath* copyright © 2003 by Lauren F. Winner
*Mudhouse Sabbath Study Edition* copyright © 2015 by Lauren F. Winner

ISBN: 978-1-61261-453-3

The names and identifying details of a few of the people who appear in these pages have been changed.

Library of Congress Cataloging-in-Publication Data

Winner, Lauren F.
  Mudhouse Sabbath : an invitation to a life of spiritual discipline / Lauren F. Winner. — STUDY EDITION.
      pages cm
  Includes bibliographical references.
  Originally published: c2003.
  ISBN 978-1-61261-453-3
  1. Winner, Lauren F. 2. Judaism—Liturgy. 3. Anglican Communion—Liturgy. 4. Anglican converts—United States—Biography. 5. Christian converts from Judaism—United States—Biography. I. Title.
  BV2623.W56A3 2015
  248.4'6—dc23                                                                                          2015015675


10  9 8 7 6 5 4 3 2 1

Published by Paraclete Press
Brewster, Massachusetts
www.paracletepress.com
Printed in the United States of America

# CONTENTS

# INTRODUCTION
## to the Study Edition

T he book you are reading was conceived fourteen years ago, not long after my conversion from Judaism to Christianity. I was enraptured by the church and everything I was learning as a new Christian about all that I might do to notice, hear from, and be pulled more fully into friendship with God. I was captivated by the Lord's Prayer, Eucharist, *lectio divina*. At the same time, I missed much about my life as an observant Jew. There was a certain religious choreography in observant Judaism that drew me into a daily awareness of God and of the holy. I found I missed the way Jewish practice helped create sacred space in my home, and the way Jewish practice connected even the most mundane actions, like eating, to life with God.

*Mudhouse Sabbath* began as a meditation on those things I missed. As I wrote, I realized that many of the Jewish spiritual practices I missed were not incompatible with life as a Christian—indeed, many of them were part of the deep structure of Christianity, too: Judaism and Christianity, for example, both name prayer as a place where we can encounter (and be encountered by) God. Both traditions name Sabbath-keeping as a way to dwell non-productively with God. And so the book changed shape a bit, becoming less a bundle of nostalgia and yearning, and more a reflection on a set of spiritual practices that, in fact, organize both Judaism and Christianity. The question I sought to answer was "What can Christians learn from Judaism about these practices that structure both our traditions, and what can Christians learn from Judaism about the God we both worship?"

Of course, my life with God, and my thinking about religious practice, has grown and changed in the last decade and a half. Today, when I open *Mudhouse Sabbath*, I notice that, if their wholesale absence from this book is any indicator, categories and questions that are important to my thinking today were not on my mind at all years ago. Most centrally, the idea that pursuing God's justice in the world, and expecting to encounter God while doing so, has become important to my spiritual life, and to my understanding of what life as a disciple of Jesus entails, but I say virtually nothing about it in this book. That silence was most obvious to me while rereading two chapters: fasting and Sabbath. So, as you read the fasting chapter in this new edition, I ask you to hold in mind a question that you won't find addressed there: how does temporarily, voluntarily abstaining from food connect us not only with God, but also with those who have too little food? How, in other words, is fasting an act of solidarity with hungry people—people who live in the cracks and crevices of society, people for whom Jesus seems to have a special fondness? This notion that fasting quickens rich people's sympathies for poor people is, by the way, something that Jewish and Christian tradition have discussed over the centuries—a discussion often prompted by God's question, in Isaiah:

> Is not this the fast that I choose:
>     to loose the bonds of injustice,
>     to undo the thongs of the yoke,

to let the oppressed go free,
  and to break every yoke?
Is it not to share your bread with the hungry,
  and bring the homeless poor into your house;
when you see the naked, to cover them,
  and not to hide yourself from your own kin?
[Isa. 58:6–7]

"Fasting can heighten our sense of solidarity with the destitute and the hungry throughout the world," sums up Rabbi Samuel M. Stahl. Thus, right around the great Jewish fast of Yom Kippur, people frequently give extra money or food to charities—to testify to, and act on, that awakened compassion.

Justice is absent from the Sabbath chapter, too. These days, when I think about Sabbath and rest, I am more aware than I once was that there are many people in our society who do not have the luxury of wringing their hands over whether they are or are not keeping Sabbath. I am more aware of the working poor who may be holding down two or three jobs, working all through the weekend, and even so are barely able to keep food on the table. Practicing Sabbath is a faithful way to look for God—and, at the very same time, for Christians in North America, practicing Sabbath may be a mark of the practitioner's comfort and privilege. Here, too, is a lesson from Judaism. Judaism suggests that one's weekly day of rest should transform the rest of the week. As Joseph of Hamadan wrote:

The Sabbath day is a soul for the other six days; they derive their nourishment . . . from it. It is at the center, the essence and foundation of all. It is the middle stem of the candelabrum, upon whose [energy] the six candles draw. So the Sabbath is in the middle: Sunday, Monday, and Tuesday are called the 'Conclusion of Shabbat' and Wednesday, Thursday and Friday are called 'Sabbath eve.' The Sabbath is in the middle, imparting [light and Divine presence] to the six days of activity.

It seems to me that if you and I are going to integrate the rhythms of Sabbath rest into our lives, one way weekly rest should change our other six days is this: we should devote ourselves, during our six work days, to working for a world of just labor practices, a world in which everyone can afford to rest.

That new attention to God's justice is not the only thing that has changed in my life since I wrote the first edition of this book. Some things about my day-to-day life have changed. In these pages, you will meet my mother, sick with cancer, and you will meet a narrator (me) who professes no intimate acquaintance with death: my mother died shortly after *Mudhouse Sabbath* was published, and I was at her bedside. In these pages, you will meet the man I married eleven years ago; we are no longer married. I also weigh a little more than I did when I wrote this book, and have more gray hair than I did then, and crow's feet. And I no longer live in Charlottesville, Virginia, home to the still-wonderful Mudhouse coffee shop from which the book's title comes. I now live in North Carolina, and nowadays, I tend to avoid coffee shops and drink my coffee at home, on a small red couch by the window.

I attended divinity school after I wrote this book, and I wrote an academic tome about religious practice in eighteenth-century Virginia (it is obscure and somewhat narrow, and if you read it, you will join a club of about six people). In divinity school and in the Virginia archives, I learned more about spiritual practices that Christians in earlier eras were committed to. For example, chapter three of this book sketches the contours of mourning in Jewish communities, and suggests that contemporary Christian communities barely know how to mourn at all. To a large extent, I would say the exact same thing today—but I would add something I have learned in the last decade: in earlier centuries, Christian communities had robust practices of mourning and bereavement, which accomplished much the same thing that Jewish mourning practices accomplish. For example, Jews inhabit a yearlong calendar of mourning, with mourners praying a specific prayer, the mourner's *kaddish*, every day for a year. A similar calendar was once observed by bereaved Christians who wore mourning clothes for a year. Those mourning clothes were just one of a host of bereavement practices that, once commonplace in Christian community, have now been largely forgotten by the church. Learning about these earlier Christian mourning practices only deepens my sense that for Christians to take inspiration from Jewish observance of shared spiritual practices is not to borrow or poach—it is, rather, to reacquaint ourselves with our own spiritual heritage.

And yet: I have also, over the last decade, learned more about how problematic it can be for Christians to, indeed, borrow Jewish practice. The whole Christian story, in a sense, is an appropriation of the Jewish story, and there is something troubling about that appropriation. It is not *only* troubling, but troubling is one thing that it is. And so, while I believe that Christian learning from Jewish practice may yield a faithful enrichment of Christians' spiritual lives, I also feel more cautious about that learning and borrowing and taking inspiration from—because over the centuries the church has taken much from Judaism, and taken it in the wrong key. At a minimum, it seems to me that our Christian learning from Judaism needs to be approached with humility and care, and as much as possible it should be undertaken while listening to Jewish friends' and neighbors' reactions and responses and thoughts about the whole project—the project of Christians learning about Judaism not primarily so that they understand Judaism better, but so that they might deepen their own Christian spiritual practice.

Here is a small secret: originally this book was going to have twelve chapters, but I got really, really behind, and so . . . the book has eleven chapters. The twelfth chapter was supposed to be on tithing, and I still believe that Christians have a lot to learn from Judaism about tithing—not just that we "should" give away ten percent of our income, but that we are doing so only secondarily to keep the lights on in the church, to keep the pastor paid, to keep the shelves at our favorite food bank stocked. We give away money because doing so can transform our relationship with God, and with the created world.

So there could be a twelfth chapter on tithing, or there could be other wonderful twelfth chapters: what do Christians have to learn from Judaism about silence? About solitude and community? About love? About forgiveness? About intimacy with God?

And yet, there is, in this edition of the book, no new twelfth chapter. Instead, throughout this edition threads an invitation to a (twelfth) spiritual practice that is central to both Judaism and Christianity: study.

Both Judaism and Christianity—drawing foremost on the commandment in Deuteronomy 6 to love God not only with your soul and heart and strength, but also with your mind— understand study as spiritual practice. Studying the Scriptures or other sacred texts, attentive reading of theology, even the study of the history of one's faith tradition—all of that can be a virtuous spiritual practice that might knit you into closer, more honest relationship with God and with your neighbor. In my own life, this is a lesson I learned first in Judaism, just as I first learned the wisdom and beauty of Sabbath, song, and penance first in Judaism. Some members of the Jewish community in which I lived set aside time each day, others each week, to carefully study a few lines of the Talmud (an ancient collection of rabbinic interpretation of the Bible—see the glossary). When I say a few lines, I mean a few lines: occasionally, several hours could be devoted to drinking in the meaning of just two or three words. This study happened *b'chevruta*, in pairs. I found this studying as part of a pair challenging at first—I am pretty solitary, and especially when my nose is in a book, I want to be alone. But over time I came to see the wisdom of organizing text study in pairs: when I meet with you to study a sacred text, I am acknowledging the limits of my own resources; I am acknowledging that the people of God listen to God's revelation in Scripture together, and that the meaning I find in the text must always be held next to the meaning you find—or, indeed, next to the meaning that we find together. And when I study text with you, I am acknowledging, also, that I come to this text not only to meet God or to learn to love God more fully, but also to meet and love you.

Although I learned about the practice of text study first from Judaism, it is of course true that study is also central to Christian faith and practice. For many of us, the most important study is Bible study—often pursued in a group, sometimes pursued alone. Shot through the Scriptures is the imperative to study the Scriptures—as in the beginning of Psalm 1: "Happy are those . . . [whose] delight is in the law of the LORD, and on his law they meditate day and night" (v. 1–2). But it is not just Scripture that we study; we study the whole of the Christian tradition—theology and church history. (Our study of biology and Jane Austen and architecture can be spiritual practice, too. Studying *Pride and Prejudice* is, of course, not the same as studying the Bible, but we can nonetheless see it as part of our Christian spiritual lives, our lives lived before God—both because we trust that God can show us something about human nature, about ourselves, about social arrangements when we read *Pride and Prejudice*; and because we trust that it is God's renewal of our minds that allows us to apprehend whatever is good and true and beautiful inside Austen's words.)

So the twelfth chapter of this book is not a chapter, but an invitation on each page to study—to study what the Scriptures, and wise Christian and Jewish teachers, have to say about Sabbath, and bereavement, and fasting. In each chapter you will find teachings from the tradition decorating the margins of the pages, and you will find a few passages clustered at the end of each chapter. To some of these teachings, I have appended questions for your pondering or discussion.

I am writing these words in my office at Duke Divinity School, and there is a certain irony to writing, from this office on this corridor, about the "study" of religious texts, religious books. We are in the fourth week of the semester, and the students are "studying" a lot—but mostly, I suspect, they are skimming. The same must be said of their professors, or at least of me: yesterday I "read" three books, but of course I didn't really read them; I raced through them, trying to find the information I needed (which I will ultimately deposit in the book I am writing, which will in turn be raced through and cannibalized by other people).

This kind of skimming is not what Christianity has historically envisioned when it has enjoined study of the Scripture and of other edifying texts. Christianity has envisioned a slow, ruminating, digestive reading—as captured in these words by the eleventh-century theologian Anselm of Canterbury:

> Taste the goodness of your Redeemer, burn with love for your Savior. Chew the honeycomb of his words, suck their flavor, which is more pleasing than honey, swallow their health-giving sweetness. Chew by thinking, suck by understanding, swallow by loving and rejoicing. Be happy in chewing, be grateful in sucking, delight in swallowing.

That readerly injunction may seem odd to us twenty-first-century readers, not only because we are unaccustomed to thinking of reading in alimentary terms, but also because no one has time to delight in reading. Even the reading we do for pleasure, rather than for work and school—the novel we're reading for our book club, say—often feels like something we have squeezed into an overfull day or week. Even our Bible study can feel squeezed in and hurried. I hope you will feel free to read every word of this book, if you wish—but I also hope you will feel free to read just seventeen words, or 100, or 306. Maybe one small passage that I quote from the Bible or the Talmud or from a modern-day rabbi or priest will grab your attention; if so, feel free to stay with those words, to chew them, to reflect on them, to learn them and let them learn you.

That is a way of saying that I am inviting you to study and be studied, rather than to skim. You can study in a group, or with a friend, *b'chevruta*. You can even study alone, but you won't really be alone, because you will be in the company of the voices that now decorate this book's pages; the rabbis and pastors and writers and scholars whose insights and questions you will encounter on the margins of these pages will be studying alongside you, as, in a sense, will I.

Lauren F. Winner
Epiphany 2015

# INTRODUCTION
## to the First Edition

If you call my friend Molly and no one is home, you will be greeted by an answering machine that asks, in the voice of Molly's six-year-old son, that you "please tell us your story."

Here's my story, in a nutshell: I grew up at a synagogue in a small college town in Virginia. (Congregation Beth Israel in Charlottesville, to be precise.) At sixteen, I went off to college in New York City. And then, near the end of college, I converted to Christianity. A few years later I moved back to the small college town in Virginia. Now I worship at a gray stone church that boasts a lovely rose window and a breaking-down organ and the most dedicated team of Sunday-school teachers in the South. Here at Christ Episcopal Church, I understand what people mean when they toss around that phrase "my church home." Christ Episcopal Church, incidentally, is exactly two blocks away from Congregation Beth Israel.

It is now going on seven years since I converted from Judaism to Christianity, and I am still in that blissed-out newlywed stage in which you can't believe your good fortune and you know that this person (in this case Jesus) whom you have chosen (or, in this case, who has chosen you) is the best person on the whole planet and you wouldn't take all the tea in China or a winning Lotto ticket or even a nice country estate in exchange.

Still, I miss Jewish ways. I miss the rhythms and routines that drew the sacred down into the everyday. I miss Sabbaths on which I actually rested. I have even found that I miss the drudgery of keeping kosher. I miss the work these practices effected between me and God.

∾

This is a book about those things I miss. It is about Sabbaths and weddings and burials and prayers, rituals Jews and Christians both observe, but also rituals we observe quite differently. It is about paths to the God of Israel that both Jews and Christians travel. It is, to be blunt, about spiritual practices that Jews do better. It is, to be blunter, about Christian practices that would be enriched, that would be thicker and more vibrant, if we took a few lessons from Judaism. It is ultimately about places where Christians have some things to learn.

Jews do these things with more attention and wisdom not because they are more righteous nor because God likes them better, but rather because doing, because action, sits at the center of Judaism. Practice is to Judaism what belief is to Christianity. That is not to say that Judaism doesn't have dogma or doctrine. It is rather to say that for Jews, the essence of the thing is a doing, an action. Your faith might come and go, but your practice ought not waver. (Indeed, Judaism suggests that the repeating of the practice is the best way to ensure that a doubter's faith will return.) This is perhaps best explained by a *midrash* (a rabbinic commentary on a biblical text). This *midrash* explains a curious turn of phrase in the Book of Exodus: *"Na'aseh v'nishma,"* which means "we will do and we will hear" or "we will do and we will understand," a phrase drawn from Exodus 24, in which the people of Israel proclaim "All the words that God has spoken, we will do and we will hear." The word order, the rabbis have observed, doesn't seem to make any sense: How can a person obey God's commandment before they hear it? But the counter-intuitive lesson, the *midrash* continues, is precisely that one acts out God's commands, one does things unto God, and eventually, through the doing, one will come to hear and understand and believe. In this *midrash*, the rabbis have offered an apology for spiritual practice, for doing.

"Spiritual practice" is a phrase that means what it says. Madeline L'Engle once likened spiritual practice to piano etudes: You do not necessarily enjoy the etudes—you want to skip right ahead to the sonatas and concertos—but if you don't work through the etudes you will arrive at the sonatas and not know what to do. So, too, with the spiritual life. It's not all about mountaintops. Mostly it's about training so that you'll know the mountaintop for what it is when you get there.

All religions have spiritual practices. Buddhists burn sage and meditate. Muslims avail themselves of their prayer rugs. Christian tradition has developed a wealth of practices, too: fasting, almsgiving, vigil-keeping, confessing, meditating. True enough, Christians in America—especially Protestants in America—have not historically practiced those practices with much discipline, but that is beginning to change. In churches and homes everywhere people are increasingly interested in *doing* Christianity, not just speaking or believing it. Here is the place where so-called Jewish-Christian relations become practical. If the church wants to grow in its attendance to, in its doing of things for the God of Israel, we might want to take a few tips from the Jewish community.

There are, of course, some key differences between how Jews and Christians understand the doing of practice (differences that are perhaps most succinctly captured with Paul's words: "Christ, and him crucified"). The Jewish practices I wish to translate into a Christian idiom are binding upon Jews. Jews are obligated to fulfill the particularities of Mosaic law. They don't light Sabbath candles simply because candles make them feel close to God, but because God commanded the lighting of candles: Closeness might be a nice by-product, but it is not the point.

Christians will understand candle-lighting a little differently. Spiritual practices don't justify us. They don't save us. Rather, they refine our Christianity; they make the inheritance Christ gives us on the Cross more fully our own. The spiritual disciplines—such as regular prayer, and fasting, and tithing, and attentiveness to our bodies—can form us as Christians through-out our lives. Are we obligated to observe these disciplines? Not generally, no. Will they get us into heaven? They will not.

Practicing the spiritual disciplines does not make us Christians. Instead, the practicing teaches us what it means to live as Christians. (There is an etymological clue here—*discipline* is related to the word *disciple.*) The ancient disciplines form us to respond to God, over and over always, in gratitude, in obedience, and in faith. Herewith, a small book of musings on and explorations in those practices.

*Na'aseh v'nishma.*

# ONE

# Shabbat

## Sabbath

R ecently, at a used bookstore, I came across Nan Fink's memoir *Stranger in the Midst*, the story of her conversion to Judaism. She describes the preparations she and her soon-to-be-husband made for Shabbat:

> On Friday afternoon, at the very last minute, we'd rush home, stopping at the grocery to pick up supplies. Flying into the kitchen we'd cook ahead for the next twenty-four hours. Soup and salad, baked chicken, yams and applesauce for dinner, and vegetable cholent or lasagna for the next day's lunch. Sometimes I'd think how strange it was to be in such a frenzy to get ready for a day of rest.
>
> Shabbat preparations had their own rhythm, and once the table was set and the house straightened, the pace began to slow. "It's your turn first in the shower," I'd call to Michael. "Okay, but it's getting late," he'd answer, concerned about starting Shabbat at sunset.
>
> In the bathroom I'd linger at the mirror, examining myself, stroking the little lines on my face, taking as much time as I could to settle into a mood of quietness. When I joined Michael and his son for the lighting of the candles, the whole house

> **THE SABBATH** is the dream of perfection . . . the sign
> of Creation and the first revelation . . . the anticipation of
> redemption. . . . Indeed, on the Sabbath the congregation
> feels as if it were already redeemed.
> —FRANZ ROSENZWEIG

*seemed transformed. Papers and books were neatly piled, flowers stood in a vase on the table, and the golden light of the setting sun filled the room. . . .*

*Shabbat is like nothing else. Time as we know it does not exist for these twenty-four hours, and the worries of the week soon fall away. A feeling of joy appears. The smallest object, a leaf or a spoon, shimmers in a soft light, and the heart opens. Shabbat is a meditation of unbelievable beauty.*

I was sitting with a cup of hot chai in a red velvet chair at the Mudhouse, a coffee shop in Charlottesville, when I read that passage. It was a Sunday afternoon. I had attended church in the morning, then cleaned out my car, then read *Those Can-Do Pigs* with my friend's two-year-old twins, and eventually wended my way down to the Mudhouse for chai and a half hour with a good book. It was not an ordinary workday, and I did feel somewhat more relaxed than I would on Monday morning. But it was not Shabbat. Nan Fink nailed it: Shabbat is like nothing else. And Shabbat is, without question, the piece of Judaism I miss the most.

It is also the piece I should most easily be able to keep. A yearning to, say, observe the Jewish new year, or a desire to hear the Torah chanted in Hebrew: Those things might be harder to incorporate into a Christian life. But the Sabbath! The Sabbath is a basic unit of Christian time, a day the Church, too, tries to devote to reverence of God and rest from toil. And yet here a Sunday afternoon finds me sitting in a coffee shop, spending money, scribbling in the margins of my book, very much in "time as we know it," not at all sure that I have opened my heart in any particular way.

God first commands the Sabbath to the Jewish people in Exodus, with the initial revelation of the Ten Commandments, and then again in Deuteronomy. The two iterations are similar, though not identical. In Exodus God says, *"Remember the Sabbath day and keep it holy,"* whereas in Deuteronomy He enjoins us to *"observe* the Sabbath day and keep it holy."* Elsewhere in the Hebrew Bible, God elaborates upon this simple instruction, noting in Exodus 35, for example, that no fire should be kindled on Shabbat, and in Isaiah 66 that on the Sabbath, the faithful should "come to worship before me."

There are, in Judaism, two types of commandments (*mitzvot*): the *mitzvot asei,* or the "Thou shalts," and the *mitzvot lo ta'aseh,* or the "Thou shalt nots." Sabbath observance comprises both. You are commanded, principally, to be joyful and restful on Shabbat, to hold great feasts, sing happy hymns, dress in

---

**IN THE END,** all will be Sabbath.

—ELLIOT K. GINSBURG

---

your finest. Married couples even get rabbinical brownie points for having sex on the Sabbath.

And then, of course, are the *mitzvot lo ta'aseh*. The cornerstone of Jewish Sabbath observance is the prohibition of work in Exodus 20 and Deuteronomy 5: "You shall not do any work, you or your son or your daughter, your male or female servant or your cattle or your sojourner who stays with you." Over time, the rabbis teased out of the text just what the prohibition on work meant, first identifying thirty-nine categories of activities to be avoided on Shabbat, and then fleshing out the implications of those thirty-nine (if one is not to light a fire, for example, one also ought not handle matches or kindling).

It's easy to look at the Jewish Sabbath as a long list of thou shalt nots: Don't turn on lights; don't drive; don't cook; don't carry a pair of scissors anywhere at all (for if you carry them you might be tempted to use them, and cutting is also forbidden on Shabbat); it's okay to carry a stone or a sweater or a scarf, but only inside your own house, not out onto the street and then into the house of another; don't plan for the week ahead; don't write a sonnet or a sestina or a haiku; don't even copy down a recipe; and while you are allowed to sing, you shouldn't play a musical instrument, and of course you mustn't turn on a radio or a record player. What all this boils down to (and boiling is another thing you cannot do on Shabbat) is *do not create.* Do not create a casserole or a Valentine card or a symphony or a pot

**WITH THE SABBATH-SOUL**, all sadness and anger are forgotten. Joy reigns on high and below.

—A KABBALISTIC TEACHING

of coffee. Do not create anything at all, for one of the things the Sabbath reprises is God's rest after He finished creating.

One of the finest explanations I know of the Orthodox Sabbath comes from Lis Harris's *Holy Days,* a journalistic ethnography of a Hasidic family in Crown Heights, New York. Harris, a secular Jew, has come to Crown Heights to spend Shabbat with the Konigsbergs. She is perplexed, and a little annoyed, by all the restrictions. Over dinner, she asks her hosts why God cares whether or not she microwaves a frozen dinner on Friday night. "What happens when we stop working and controlling nature?" Moishe Konigsberg responds. "When we don't operate machines, or pick flowers, or pluck fish from the sea? . . . When we cease interfering in the world we are acknowledging that it is God's world."

∽

I remember, from my Jewish days, the language we used to name the Sabbath. We spoke of the day as *Shabbat haMalka,* the Sabbath Queen, and we sang hymns of praise on Friday night that welcomed the Sabbath as a bride. It is something of this reverence, and this celebration, that is missing from my Sabbaths now.

I remember the end of Shabbat, Saturday night. By the time Saturday night rolls around, part of you is eager to hop in your car and race to a movie, go out dancing, sip a late-night espresso. But still, even after a full day of Shabbat rest and even Shabbat toe-tapping boredom (because, let's face it, occasionally Shabbat gets dull), even then you are sad to see Shabbat go. You mark the end of Shabbat with a ceremony called *havdalah,* which comes from the Hebrew verb meaning "to separate," in this case

**IN HER ARTICLE** "The Sabbath: The Culmination of Creation," Old Testament scholar Ellen F. Davis writes:

A 70 hour work week, a car phone and a beeper that make us accessible at every moment—for us, these are status symbols; though, from a different perspective, they might be seen as signs of oppression. But the Sabbath commandment—the most frequently reiterated of all 613 commandments in the Bible—demands that we break the habit of constant busyness. Far from congratulating us on the ability to keep working despite physical, mental and emotional exhaustion, the Bible declares that the failure to set appropriate limits on work is a criminal offense of the highest order: "Whoever profanes [the Sabbath] will surely be put to death. Indeed, everyone who does work on it, that soul (Hebrew nefesh) is to be cut off from among her people" (Ex 31:14b). The workaholic falls under the death penalty, which ancient Israel reserved for the gravest crimes against God and humanity.

separating Shabbat from the week. *havdalah* involves a number of ritual objects—wine for tasting, and a braided candle for lighting, and a box of fragrant spices (cloves, often, and cinnamon), and you pass around the spice box because smelling the sweet spices comforts you a little, you who are sad that Shabbat has ended. One of the reasons you are sad is this: Judaism speaks of a *neshamah yeteirah,* an extra soul that comes to dwell in you on the Sabbath but departs once the week begins.

I remember that, for Jews, the Sabbath shapes all the rhythms of calendar and time; the entire week points toward Shabbat. The rabbis, who are always interested in the subtleties of Torah prose, puzzled over the two different versions of the Sabbath commandment. Why, in Exodus, does God tell us to *remember* the Sabbath, whereas in Deuteronomy He instructs *observance* of the Sabbath? One story the rabbis tell about the difference between remembrance and observance has to do with ordering time. Sunday, Monday, and Tuesday are caught up in remembering the preceding Shabbat, while Wednesday through Friday are devoted to preparing for the next Shabbat.

What, really, was wrong with my Mudhouse Sabbath? After all, I did spend Sunday morning in church. And I wasn't *working* that afternoon, not exactly.

A fine few hours, except that my Sunday was more an afternoon off than a Sabbath. It was an add-on to a busy week, not the fundamental unit around which I organized my life. The Hebrew word for *holy* means, literally, "set apart." In failing to live a Sabbath truly distinct from weekly time, I had violated a most basic command: to keep the Sabbath holy.

I am not suggesting that Christians embrace the strict regulations of the Orthodox Jewish Sabbath. Indeed, the New Testament unambiguously inaugurates a new understanding of

Shabbat. In his epistles, Paul makes clear that the Sabbath, like other external signs of piety, is insufficient for salvation. As he writes in his letter to the Colossians, "Therefore do not let anyone judge you . . . with regard to a religious festival, a New Moon celebration or a Sabbath day. These are a shadow of the things that were to come; the reality, however, is found in Christ." And Jesus, when rebuked by the Pharisees for plucking grain from a field on Shabbat, criticizes those who would make a fetish of Sabbath observance, insisting that "the Sabbath was made for man, not man for the Sabbath."

But there is something, in the Jewish Sabbath that is absent from most Christian Sundays: a true cessation from the rhythms of work and world, a time wholly set apart, and, perhaps above all, a sense that the point of Shabbat, the orientation of Shabbat, is toward God.

Pick up any glossy women's magazine from the last few years and you'll see what I mean. The Sabbath has come back into fashion, even among the most secular Americans, but the Sabbath we now embrace is a curious one. Articles abound extolling the virtues of treating yourself to a day of rest, a relaxing and leisurely visit to the spa, an extra-long bubble bath, and a glass of Chardonnay. *Take a day off,* the magazines urge their harried readers. *Rest.*

There might be something to celebrate in this revival of Sabbath, but it seems to me that there are at least two flaws in the reasoning. First is what we might call capitalism's justification for Sabbath rest: resting one day a week makes you more productive during the other six. Or, as my father has often told me, I'll get more done working eleven months a year than twelve. And while that may be true, rest for the sake of future productivity is at odds with the spirit of Shabbat.

**WHAT DO YOU MAKE** of the Sabbath commandment's being the "most frequently reiterated" of all the Old Testament commandments? Reflect on Davis's observation that "Far from congratulating us on the ability to keep working despite physical, mental and emotional exhaustion, the Bible declares that the failure to set appropriate limits on work is a criminal offense of the highest order": what might the biblical imperative to set appropriate work limits call us to as a society? What might it call you to as an individual? How might your church community respond to the Bible's call to set limits on work?

We could call the second problem with the current Sabbath vogue the fallacy of the direct object. Whom is the contemporary Sabbath designed to honor? Whom does it benefit? Why, the bubble-bath taker herself, of course! The Bible suggests something different. In observing the Sabbath, one is both giving a gift to God and imitating Him. Exodus and Deuteronomy make this clear when they say, "Six days shall you labor and do all your work. But the seventh day is a sabbath to the LORD your God." *To the LORD your God.*

❧

Christianity, of course, has a long tradition of Sabbath observance, so a revitalized Sabbath is more a reclaiming of the Christian birthright than the self-conscious adoption of something Jewish. Jesus observed Shabbat, even as He challenged the specifics of Mosaic Sabbath law; and since at least the year 321, when Constantine declared Sunday as Sabbath for all his empire, Christians have understood the Sabbath as a day for rest, communal worship, and celebration. New England Puritans summed up their thoughts about Sunday thus: "Good Sabbaths make good Christians."

For Christians, the Sabbath has an added dimension: It commemorates not only God's resting from Creation, but also God's Resurrection. As eighteenth-century Pietist Johann Friedrich Starck put it, "Under the New Testament, Christians also consecrate one day out of seven, Sunday, to God, that being the day on which Christ rose from the dead, and the Holy Spirit was poured out." (Starck encouraged readers even to begin their Sabbath practices on Saturday evening, urging the Christian to "disentangle his mind from worldly cares and troubles . . . Prepare himself for the coming Sunday with prayer, . . . [and] Retire to rest betimes," so as to be punctual and sprightly at church the next morning.)

As for me, I am starting small. I have joined a Bible study that meets Sundays at five, a bookend to my day that helps me live into Shabbat—there's not enough time between church and Bible study to pull out my laptop and start working, so instead I try to have a leisurely lunch with friends from church. I have forsworn Sunday shopping (a bigger sacrifice than you may realize), and I sometimes join my friend Ginger on her afternoon visits to church shut-ins. Sometimes before Bible study, you will find me with the twins and the can-do pigs, and sometimes still you will find me at the Mudhouse. Not much, when compared to the dramatic cessations of the Orthodox Shabbat; but still, the first arcs of a return to Sabbath.

**LEVITICUS TELLS US** that the earth, the soil, is meant to experience Sabbath rest: "For six years sow your fields, and for six years prune your vineyards and gather their crops. But in the seventh year the land is to have a year of sabbath, a sabbath to the LORD. Do not sow your fields or prune your vineyards. Do not reap what grows of itself or harvest the grapes of your untended vines. The land is to have a year of rest. Whatever the land yields during the sabbath year will be food for you—for yourself, your male and female servants, and the hired worker and temporary resident who live among you, as well as for your livestock and the wild animals in your land. Whatever the land produces may be eaten." (Lev. 25:3–7, NIV)

Theologian Norman Wirzba explains that "Here we find roughly parallel requirements for the provision of food, as well as rest, for humans and nonhumans alike. Our Sabbath rest must not be at the expense of another's toil or misery; we must exercise care to make sure that the alien and the household servant, but also animals and the land itself, are properly nourished and cared for." When you imagine giving the earth a Sabbath, what do you see? What impact would this on your daily life or actions?

The passage in Leviticus also spells out that the Israelites' male and female servants are to have a Sabbath. Most of us don't have male and female servants today—but low-wage earners in fact serve me all the time. Men and women earning low wages empty the trashcan of my office, for example. And when I go to a restaurant for lunch after church—aren't the cook and the waitress serving me? What am I doing—and what are you doing—to help create a Sabbath for those men and women?

**"SABBATH, SEVENTH DAY OF CREATION:** God rested. We are to close out the workaday world for a little while. But how? In the traditional mode, women provide the means. In practice, there are dishes to wash and beds to make and babies to change and children to run after at synagogue and meals to set out after the Friday sun slips behind the rising earth and during that rotation of earth and glimpse of moon we know as Saturday. Only a man, and a rare man today, would say that this is not 'work' next to driving a car or flipping a light switch—actions proscribed in the strictest readings. The vernacular has it both ways.

When you light your candles and say *Kiddush*, you 'welcome' the Sabbath. The Sabbath arrives, and you celebrate. When you wash your floor, dust, cook, and set the table on Friday, however, you 'make' Sabbath.

So, what exactly is it that women do? Are women God? Does the Sabbath exist independently from the preparations, from the tradition? Can you meet your family for a pizza dinner on Friday, relax together for the first time all week, drive home after dark, snuggle up to a video tape, feel happy to be alive, and call it *Shabbas*? . . . The rabbis rather firmly say no. A tired man and woman might prefer yes."

—ELIZABETH ERLICH

# Discussion Questions

**1.** A crucial piece of Jewish Sabbath observance is abstaining from work. Consider the following rabbinic exegesis of several scriptural passages about Shabbat (the biblical texts under consideration are in capital letters): "SIX DAYS YOU SHALL LABOR AND DO ALL YOUR WORK" (Ex. 20:9). Can a human being possibly complete all his work in six days? Rather cease from work as if it had all been completed. Another interpretation: Cease from even thinking about work. Thus it says "IF YOU REFRAIN FROM TRAMPLING THE SABBATH, FROM PURSUING YOUR AFFAIRS ON MY HOLY DAY; IF YOU CALL THE SABBATH 'DELIGHT,' THE LORD'S HOLY DAY 'HONORED'; AND YOU HONOR IT AND GO NOT YOUR WAYS NOR LOOK TO YOUR AFFAIRS, NOR STRIKE BARGAINS" — (Isa. 58:13) and "THEN YOU CAN SEEK THE FAVOR OF THE LORD" (Isa. 58:14). This text acknowledges that all work can never be accomplished in six days. What would it mean for you, personally, to "cease from work as if it had all been completed" in order to rest on the Sabbath? Do you ever feel that you have "completed" all that you have to do? Do you think it is possible to truly "Cease from even thinking about work?" Why or why not? What patterns do you have in your day-to-day life that make it difficult to stop working—that make it difficult to even stop thinking about working?

**2.** The weekly rhythm of the Sabbath is meant to create a pattern of work and rest that is sustainable and God-honoring. I write that "for Jews, the Sabbath shapes all the rhythms of calendar and time; the entire week points toward Shabbat" (page 7). Now, consider this quotation from Rabbi Elazar ben Hananiah: "Remember the Sabbath day continually from the first day of the week. If a good portion happens to come your way, prepare it for use on the Sabbath." What might it look like to consider, and prepare for, the coming of the Sabbath all week long? How would it change your understanding of the other six days of the week to know that you are looking ahead to a day of rest?

I also note that "Judaism speaks of a neshamah yeteirah, an extra soul that comes to dwell in you on the Sabbath but departs once the week begins" (page 7). A passage from the Talmud comments on this "extra soul": "For Resh Lakish said: An additional soul is given to man on Friday and remains with him for the duration of Shabbat. At the conclusion of Shabbat that additional soul is taken away from him, leaving him weakened and sad." Why might you—your weekday soul—feel weakened and sad by the departure of Sabbath? What does rest do for your soul that working cannot do?

∽

**3.** Saint Augustine, a fourth- and fifth-century Christian theologian and bishop, writes that observing the Sabbath
"imposes a regular periodical holiday—quietness of heart,
tranquility of mind, the product of a good conscience. Here is
sanctification, because here is the Spirit of God." What does
observance of Sabbath, this "regular periodical holiday," have
to do with conscience? Do you think that taking a day of rest
would change you? Why or why not?

**4.** Jesus speaks about the Sabbath in the Gospel of Mark:

> One sabbath he was going through the grainfields; and
> as they made their way his disciples began to pluck
> heads of grain. The Pharisees said to him, "Look, why
> are they doing what is not lawful on the sabbath?" And
> he said to them, "Have you never read what David did
> when he and his companions were hungry and in need of
> food? He entered the house of God, when Abiathar was
> high priest, and ate the bread of the Presence, which it
> is not lawful for any but the priests to eat, and he gave
> some to his companions." Then he said to them, "The
> sabbath was made for humankind, and not humankind
> for the sabbath; so the Son of Man is lord even of the
> sabbath." [Mk. 2:23–28]

What does Jesus mean when he says "The Sabbath was
made for man, not man for the Sabbath"? Jesus calls himself

"lord of the Sabbath." How does taking a day away from work better orient our lives and hearts around Jesus?

**5.** In the nineteenth century, a new word appeared, first in England, and then in America: weekend. At first, "weekend" denoted a day and a half—late Saturday and all day Sunday. Within a few decades, it had come to refer to both Saturday and Sunday. Aside from length, what is the difference between enjoying a weekend and keeping Sabbath? What would you lose if you traded part of the weekend for Sabbath? What might you gain?

# TWO

# Kashrut
### Fitting Food

Eating attentively is hard for me. I'm single, I'm busy, and I just don't give very much thought to what I eat. My most beloved cooking implement is the microwave. I hate going to the grocery store. I like picking up Thai food. Once in a while, I do a real doozy in the kitchen—risotto with portobello mushrooms, some sophisticated salad, chocolate mousse. But these bursts of culinary bravado are occasional and almost always designed to impress a guest.

As a practicing Jew, I kept kosher—which is to say I observed *kashrut,* the Jewish dietary laws. Keeping kosher cultivates a profound attentiveness to food. Because I kept kosher (the word comes from the Hebrew for "fit" or "appropriate"), I thought about the food I ate. I thought about what I was going to eat, and where I was going to procure it, and how I was going to prepare it. Eating was never obvious. Food required intention.

Only after I stopped keeping kosher did I fully appreciate that *kashrut* had shaped more than my grocery lists. It also shaped my spiritual life. Keeping kosher transforms eating from a mere nutritional necessity into an act of faithfulness. If you keep kosher, the protagonist of your meal is not you; it is God.

**ANITA DIAMANT HAS WRITTEN**, "Kashrut is best understood . . . as a way of sanctifying a basic need." How do dietary codes—from keeping kosher to eating seasonally—sanctify, or make holy, a basic need? In your life, currently, is the basic need of eating "sanctified"? What might sanctified eating look like? What changes in your food practices could you make to further connect food and holiness in your life?

One way of sanctifying the mundane act of eating might be to pray or explicitly try to commune with God at the table. The *Darchei Tzedek* says, "The main service of God is through eating. Moreover the *tzaddikim* (righteous ones) meditate as they eat, in love and fear of God, as with prayer." Contemporary theologian Jay Michaelson suggests that prayer after eating can also sanctify the meal. He suggests praying one line from Psalm 145: *You open your hand, and satisfy all life according to your will.* But don't just spout that sentence and bolt. Michaelson advises focusing, slowly, on each phrase: imagine a fist opening; perhaps even open your own hand. Consider what it feels like in your body to have your needs and desires satisfied.

The laws of kashrut are found in Leviticus and Deuteronomy. As with the Sabbath laws, the rabbis embroider and elaborate the dietary code in the Talmud.

There are two basic rules:

Some foods are simply forbidden: fish without both fins and scales, creepy-crawly insects, mammals that don't chew their cud and mammals that don't have cloven hooves. This means no shellfish, no porkchops, no prosciutto, no chocolate-covered ants, no lobster bisque. No bacon with your morning omelet. No Virginia ham. (All fruits and vegetables, by the way, are kosher. Eat as many chick peas, pomegranates, Bing cherries, and green beans as you want.)

Dairy products and meat products may not be eaten at the same time. The strict separation of meat and dairy is based upon Deuteronomy 14:21: "Thou shalt not seethe a kid in his mother's milk." The rabbis interpreted that verse broadly. Not only should a baby goat not be steeped, stewed, or sautéed in its mother's milk, no meat should be cooked with any dairy product. Indeed, meat and milk may not be eaten at the same meal. Nor can a pot used to cook dairy ever be used for anything *fleishig* (that's the Yiddish word for "meat," a cognate of our word "fleshy"). So forget about cheeseburgers. Forget, also, about your plan to make cream of mushroom soup in your blue stockpot tonight: Three years ago you simmered Bolognese sauce in that pot, and now it is a meat pot forever.

In addition to those two basic principles are a host of narrower rules. Never eat blood. Eat only animals that have been slaughtered according to Jewish law (the law requires the most painless slaughter possible, a quick and neat slash to the jugular vein). Don't eat an animal that has died of old age.

Curious rules indeed. But they are far from arbitrary. A cosmology and an ethics underpin each injunction; to keep kosher is to infuse the simple act of feeding oneself with meaning and consequence. The codes of *shechitah* for example—the rules that govern the ritual slaughter of animals for food—insist on compassion. Yes, we human beings have to kill other living creatures in order to eat, but let's make that killing as painless and humane as possible. Even the injunction about the kid and its mother's milk is symbolic. Rabbi Abraham Joshua Heschel observed that boiling a baby in the milk of its mother mocks the reproductive order and life itself. Rabbi Arthur Waskow has suggested that to separate meat products from milk products is to constantly recall a distinction between death (meat) and life (milk).

But one shouldn't romanticize *kashrut*. It must be admitted that *kashrut* can, at times, be a royal pain in the neck. Keeping kosher requires at least two sets of dishes, one for meat and one for dairy. You have to buy your brisket and steaks and ground round at a kosher butcher. At the grocery, you'll scrutinize packaged goods, trying to determine which are certifiably kosher (Pepperidge Farm, Ben and Jerry's, and Coca-Cola all have rabbinic sanction, and most of their products are kosher; Kraft cheddar cheese and Quaker's S'mores granola bars are not). And then there's the problem of dining with your non-Jewish friends. In their homes, or at non-kosher restaurants, you're stuck drinking water and possibly munching on raw veggies. Keeping kosher is also expensive—meat slaughtered by kosher butchers is pricey, and then there are all those extra plates. Most of all, *kashrut* requires almost constant vigilance and thought. This chicken casserole calls for cream—how can I avoid the forbidden mingling of meat and milk? (For each cup of cream,

**"*KASHRUT* CAN BE A DEEPLY SPIRITUAL PRACTICE**, especially nowadays, when it seems we can eat whatever we want whenever we want. By contrast, the Jewish dietary laws require that we consume with a measure of restraint. Before eating a meal, we have to think, *Where did this food come from? Is it from a permissible source? In the case of meat, how was it killed?*

"Dovetailing with the broader local food movement that's emerged in American culture, there's a movement underway in American Judaism that connects *kashrut* with environmentalism. Are fruits and vegetables grown with harmful pesticides that run off into streams and rivers still 'kosher'? According to traditional *halakha* [Jewish law], yes. But some see a conflict of ethical values in this scenario. If the *Torah* were written today, wouldn't God want us to consider the environmental impact of our farming practices?"

—ANDREA LIEBER

substitute a cup of chicken stock mixed with one egg yolk and a dash of cornstarch.) The *Eating Southern and Kosher* cookbook suggests that you make gumbo with tofu instead of shrimp.

❧

For Christians, this may seem quaint and intriguing but ultimately irrelevant. Throughout Christian history, interpreters have agreed that the moral precepts of the Old Testament—in particular, the Ten Commandments—are binding upon Christians, but the civil and ceremonial codes, from the dietary laws to the holiday injunctions, are not. And the New Testament rather dramatically makes clear that Christians are free to eat as many clams and oysters as they like: In the Book of Acts, a hungry Peter has a vision of a sheet of food descending from heaven. The sheet is filled with food that is both kosher and unkosher, clean and unclean—potatoes and chicken and spinach, but also pork chops and lobsters and prawns. A voice instructs Peter to "kill and eat," but Peter protests, insisting that he will never eat unclean, unkosher, food. The voice from heaven then says, "What God has made clean, you must not call profane." This story is symbolic, to be sure. The voice is talking not just about food, but also about people; the instructions are not simply to eat, but also to invite both Jews and Gentiles into the Kingdom

**"GOD HAS GIVEN** . . . all that God's people need to be able to be God's friends and to eat with him."
—SAMUEL WELLS

**"[T]HROUGH OBSERVANCE OF [KASHRUT] WE EXERCISE**, and hopefully gain control over, one of the basic activities of our lives—preparing and eating food. In effect, we are engaged in determining boundaries for ourselves within which we regulate our lives. The value of this is twofold. First, such self-control is in itself a form of personal growth. It is a paradoxical truth that through the acquisition of discipline and structure within an otherwise random and arbitrary life, freedom, spontaneity, and personal growth become possible. Second, such personal boundary-setting constantly confronts us with the knowledge and responsibility that we are, and must always be, the masters of our own lives—our selves and our bodies."

—*THE FIRST JEWISH CATALOG: A DO-IT-YOURSELF KIT*

of God. Still, the story has epicurean consequences, too. Peter, a Jew who has come to follow Christ, is free to eat any and all of those once forbidden foods.

While Christians are not bound by the particularities of deuteronomic dietary law, we may still want to pay attention to the basic principle that underlies *kashrut*: God cares about our dietary choices. This should come as no surprise; you only have to read the first two chapters of Genesis to see God's concern for food. Humanity's first sin was disobedience manifested in a choice about eating. Adam and Eve were allowed to eat anything they wanted, except the one fruit they chose. And the New Testament makes clear that God cares about the most

For me, seasonal eating is a way of incorporating more attentiveness to God with my food choices. English theologian Davit Grumett writes movingly about the spiritual fruits of seasonal eating: "By attending to the sources of our food and buying locally, we affirm the God-given network of social and ecological relationships in which we live. Attending to this network was natural in the days before mass food production and transportation. Now this connection needs to be recovered actively. By obtaining one specific item from a particular local supplier, we are more likely to feel personal gratitude in buying, preparing and eating it than if we drive to the supermarket and fill the car with goods. In ways such as these, we may use food as a means of reconnecting to . . . the seasonal calendar—which is itself God-given. We may enter more fully into the life of Christ, the doctrines about him and his sacrifices made for us. This discipline is in sharp contrast to the pick-and-mix spirituality widespread today, in which we cater to our immediate wishes." Reading Grumett's analysis, and having tried with mixed success for ten years to eat seasonally, I find myself thinking that for middle-class Americans in our current era, robust seasonal eating may in fact be the equivalent of fasting. What do you think of Grumett's argument? Do you feel persuaded? Challenged? Inspired? Unmoved?

basic, quotidian aspects of our lives. (Our God, after all, is the God who provides for the sparrows and numbers the hairs on our heads.) This God who is interested in how we speak, how we handle our money, how we carry our bodies—He is also interested in how we live with food.

At its most basic level, keeping kosher requires you to be present to your food. Of course, so does the Atkins diet. The difference between Atkins and *kashrut* is God. We try out the Atkins diet because our physician cares about what we eat. We limit ourselves to kosher food—to return to the etymology, appropriate or fitting food prepared appropriately—because God cares about what we eat.

∽

So, down to brass tacks. I am not about to stop eating shellfish again. But I am trying to bring some thought and intention to the food I eat. The impulse comes from Judaism, but for the specifics I have turned to a number of different teachers who, though not Jewish, have an intuitive appreciation for the logic of *kashrut*.

One of my food teachers is an Episcopal priest-cum-chef, Robert Farrar Capon. In 1968, Capon wrote a slender book called *The Supper of the Lamb*. It's part cookbook, part theological meditation—something like M. F. K. Fisher meets the desert fathers. (The book is, in fact, organized around a lamb recipe, and the title's biblical allusion is not accidental.)

The second chapter of *The Supper of the Lamb* begins with the slightly absurd instruction to spend "sixty minutes or so" chopping an onion. One onion, sixty minutes. The hour is to begin with the chopper looking at the onion, encountering the onion, having a "material . . . meeting" with it. After noticing its shape, its top and bottom, its blemishes, you proceed to removing its skin, moving so carefully that you do not puncture, let alone slice, the flesh of the onion itself. And on and on Capon leads us, through a veritable onion meditation. By the end of the chapter one wonders if a single hour is enough time.

What is Capon's point? Presumably not that we should all set aside sixty minutes every time we sauté a Vidalia. Rather, he is making "a case for paying attention." After an hour with your onion, you might begin to see "that the uniquenesses of creation are the result of continuous creative support, of effective regard by no mean lover." The lover of course is God. "He *likes* onions, therefore they are. The fit, the colors, the smell, the tensions, the tastes, the textures, the lines, the shapes are a response, not to some forgotten decree that there may as well be onions as turnips, but to His present delight." And so the reminders stack up on top of one another (rather, one might note, like the layers of a cake). Food is part of God's creation. A right relationship with food points us toward Him.

Another of my food teachers is Barbara Kingsolver. In an essay called "Lily's Chickens," Kingsolver explains that she eats seasonally. When tomatoes and plums are in season, she eats them. She avoids the unseasonable temptations of modern American supermarkets, which ship in greenhouse tomatoes and lemons and plums and asparagus all year round. Kingsolver only eats tomatoes in January if she canned some back in June.

Why is Kingsolver so committed to this culinary calendar? Because shipping food from greenhouses around the world is America's second-largest expenditure of oil. (The first, not surprisingly, is our daily reliance on cars.) As Kingsolver explains, "Even if you walk or bike to the store, if you come home with

**THE BAAL SHEM TOV,** the eighteenth-century rabbi who founded Hasidic Judaism, said, "[W]hen you eat, your thought should be that the taste and the sweetness of the food you are eating are coming from God's enlivening power and from the supernal sweetness which is the life of the food." What might you do during your next meal to more deeply know that your food's flavor comes from "God's enlivening power and from the supernal sweetness which is the life of the food"?

bananas from Ecuador, tomatoes from Holland, cheese from France, and artichokes from California, you have guzzled some serious gas." To eat seasonally (and locally) is to enact a politics of reduced consumption.

But seasonal eating has an almost sacramental effect as well. Though Kingsolver may not have had spiritual aims when she began eating seasonally, she nonetheless introduced a liturgical calendar to her life. Her year, just like the Jewish year or the church year, now has a rhythm. Tomatoes mean summer. Potatoes and beans suggest winter. Kingsolver's seasonal diet sacralizes not just food, but time.

I do not practice seasonal eating with the rigor I once brought to *kashrut*. Last night, for example, I found myself eating a slice of pizza topped with chunks of avocado. (It's November.)

But I have begun the move toward seasonal eating. I'm embarrassed to admit that the first step in seasonalizing my diet was study. When I read Kingsolver's essay, I realized that because I am so accustomed to Whole Foods and The Fresh Market with their year-round displays of bright, perfect produce, I had

**FOOD MATTERS TO GOD**, and how I interact with food shapes my interactions with God and with the world. While I do not plan on keeping kosher as a Christian, I do want to be intentional about what I eat as another way of keeping God at the center of my life. As author Michael Pollan has written, "'Eating is an agricultural act,' as Wendell Berry famously said. It is also an ecological act, and a political act, too. Though much has been done to obscure this simple fact, how and what we eat determines to a great extent the use we make of the world—and what is to become of it. To eat with a fuller consciousness of all that is at stake might sound like a burden, but in practice few things in life can afford quite as much satisfaction. By comparison, the pleasures of eating industrially, which is to say eating in ignorance, are fleeting." What do you think of Pollan's statement that "To eat with a fuller consciousness of all that is at stake might sound like a burden, but in practice few things in life can afford quite as much satisfaction"? Does attending consciously to your food choices seem like a burden or a delight to you? Why or why not? How might our constant busyness make eating seem like a "burden" rather than a joy? I have started a vegetable garden in the last year, and it has made eating seasonally a lot easier. What is the difference between eating seasonally when you are wholly dependent on a store for all your produce, and when you grow some of the produce in your window boxes or backyard or neighborhood garden?

no idea which fruits were in season when. I had to head to the library and read up on vegetable birthdays. (No strawberries in November, of course, but apparently persimmons are abundant here in Virginia in the fall.)

Now, like some of my Jewish friends who keep kosher at home but eat more liberally at restaurants, I try to keep a seasonal kitchen but allow myself to indulge when I'm out on the town. For the first time since I became a Christian, I have found myself thinking about what food I put in my body, and where that food has been—in whose hands, in what countries—before it got to my plate. Like Capon's musings on the onion, this reflecting on and participation with my food leads ultimately back to Him who sustains, provides, and feeds.

Seasonal eating is not for everyone, and it is certainly not the only discipline that can infuse Christian eating with attention and devotion. Some of my friends find that fasting one day a week imbues their six days of meals with a spirit of gratitude and joy. Others try to make all their food from scratch. Every loaf of bread is baked at home, every salad comprises vegetables from the garden in the backyard.

On Sunday morning as I watch my priest lay the communion table for the gathered believers, I remember why eating attentively is worth all the effort: The table is not only a place where we can become present to God. The table is also a place where He becomes present to us.

# Discussion Questions

## DEUTERONOMY 14:3–20

**YOU SHALL NOT EAT ANY ABHORRENT THING.** These are the animals you may eat: the ox, the sheep, the goat, the deer, the gazelle, the roebuck, the wild goat, the ibex, the antelope, and the mountain-sheep. Any animal that divides the hoof and has the hoof cleft in two, and chews the cud, among the animals, you may eat. Yet of those that chew the cud or have the hoof cleft you shall not eat these: the camel, the hare, and the rock badger, because they chew the cud but do not divide the hoof; they are unclean for you. And the pig, because it divides the hoof but does not chew the cud, is unclean for you. You shall not eat their meat, and you shall not touch their carcasses. Of all that live in water you may eat these: whatever has fins and scales you may eat. And whatever does not have fins and scales you shall not eat; it is unclean for you. You may eat any clean birds. But these are the ones that you shall not eat: the eagle, the vulture, the osprey, the buzzard, the kite of any kind; every raven of any kind; the ostrich, the nighthawk, the sea gull, the hawk of any kind; the little owl and the great owl, the water hen and the desert owl, the carrion vulture and the cormorant, the stork, the heron of any kind; the hoopoe and the bat. And all winged insects are unclean for you; they shall not be eaten. You may eat any clean winged creature.

LEVITICUS 11:2–32, 41–42

## SPEAK TO THE PEOPLE OF ISRAEL, SAYING:

From among all the land animals, these are the creatures that you may eat. Any animal that has divided hoofs and is cleft-footed and chews the cud—such you may eat. But among those that chew the cud or have divided hoofs, you shall not eat the following: the camel, for even though it chews the cud, it does not have divided hoofs; it is unclean for you. The rock badger, for even though it chews the cud, it does not have divided hoofs; it is unclean for you. The hare, for even though it chews the cud, it does not have divided hoofs; it is unclean for you. The pig, for even though it has divided hoofs and is cleft-footed, it does not chew the cud; it is unclean for you. Of their flesh you shall not eat, and their carcasses you shall not touch; they are unclean for you. These you may eat, of all that are in the waters. Everything in the waters that has fins and scales, whether in the seas or in the streams—such you may eat. But anything in the seas or the streams that does not have fins and scales, of the swarming creatures in the waters and among all the other living creatures that are in the waters—they are detestable to you and detestable they shall remain. Of their flesh you shall not eat, and their carcasses you shall regard as detestable. Everything in the waters that does not have fins and scales is detestable to you. These you shall regard as detestable among the birds. They shall not be eaten; they are an abomination: the eagle, the vulture, the osprey, the buzzard, the kite of any kind; every raven of any kind; the ostrich, the nighthawk, the sea gull, the hawk of any kind; the little owl, the cormorant, the great owl, the water hen, the desert owl, the carrion vulture, the stork, the heron of any kind, the hoopoe, and the bat. All winged insects that walk upon all fours are detestable to you. But among the winged insects that walk on all fours you may eat those that have jointed legs above their feet, with which to leap on the ground. Of them you may eat: the locust according to its kind, the bald locust according to its kind, the cricket according to its kind, and the grasshopper according to its kind. But all other winged insects that have four feet are detestable to you.

By these you shall become unclean; whoever touches the carcass of any of them shall be unclean until the evening, and whoever carries any part of the carcass of any of them shall wash his clothes and be unclean until the evening. Every animal that has divided hoofs but is not cleft-footed or does not chew the cud is unclean for you; everyone who touches one of them shall be unclean. All that walk on their paws, among the animals that walk on all fours, are unclean for you; whoever touches the carcass of any of them shall be unclean until the evening, and the one who carries the carcass shall wash his clothes and be unclean until the evening; they are unclean for you. These are unclean for you among the creatures that swarm upon the earth: the weasel, the mouse, the great lizard according to its kind, the gecko, the land crocodile, the lizard, the sand lizard, and the chameleon. These are unclean for you among all that swarm; whoever touches one of them when they are dead shall be unclean until the evening. And anything upon which any of them falls when they are dead shall be unclean, whether an article of wood or cloth or skin or sacking, any article that is used for any purpose; it shall be dipped into water, and it shall be unclean until the evening, and then it shall be clean. All creatures that swarm upon the earth are detestable; they shall not be eaten. Whatever moves on its belly, and whatever moves on all fours, or whatever has many feet, all the creatures that swarm upon the earth, you shall not eat; for they are detestable.

∽

**1.** Anthropologist Mary Douglas devoted many years to trying to make sense of the seemingly arbitrary Old Testament dietary laws. She carefully read the two key passages in Deuteronomy and Leviticus above, in the context of larger Old Testament discussions of holiness, and she argued this:

> Since each of the injunctions is prefaced by the command to be holy, so they must be explained by that command. There must be contrariness between holiness and abomination which will snake over-all sense of all the particular restrictions.
>
> Holiness is the attribute of Godhead. Its root means 'set apart'. What else does it mean? . . . Granted that its root means separateness, the next idea that emerges is of the Holy as wholeness and completeness. . . . Hybrids and other confusions are abominated. [H]oliness is exemplified by completeness. Holiness requires that individuals shall conform to the class to which they belong. And holiness requires that different classes of things shall not be confused. . . .
>
> We have now laid a good basis for approaching the laws about clean and unclean meats. To be holy is to be whole, to be one; holiness is unity, integrity, perfection

of the individual and of the kind. The dietary roles merely develop the metaphor of holiness on the same lines.

First we should start with livestock, the herds of cattle, camels, sheep and goats which were the livelihood of the Israelites. These animals were clean inasmuch as contact with them did not require purification before approaching the Temple. Livestock, like the inhabited land, received the blessing of God. Both land and livestock were fertile by the blessing, both were drawn into the divine order. The farmer's duty was to preserve the blessing. For one thing, he had to preserve the order of creation. So no hybrids, as we have seen, either in the fields or in the herds or in the clothes made from wool or flax. To some extent men covenanted with their land and cattle in the same way as God covenanted with them. Men respected the first born of their cattle, obliged them to keep the Sabbath. Cattle were literally domesticated as slaves. They had to be brought into the social order in order to enjoy the blessing. The difference between cattle and the wild beasts is that the wild beasts have no covenant to protect them. It is possible that the Israelites were like other pastoralists who do not relish wild game. The Nuer of the South Sudan, for instance, apply a sanction of disapproval of a man who lives by hunting. To be driven to eating wild meat is the sign of a poor herdsman. So it would be probably wrong to think of the Israelites as longing for forbidden meats and finding the restrictions irksome. Driver is surely right in taking the rules as an *a posteriori* generalisation of their habits. Cloven-hoofed, cud-chewing ungulates are the model of the proper kind of food for a pastoralist. If they must eat wild game, they can eat wild game that shares these distinctive characters and is therefore of the same general species. This is a kind of casuistry which permits scope for hunting antelope and wild goats and wild sheep. Everything would be quite straightforward were it not that the legal mind has seen fit to give ruling on some borderline cases. Some animals seem to be ruminant, such as the hare and the hyrax (or rock badger), whose constant grinding of their teeth was held to be cud-chewing. But they are definitely not cloven-hoofed and so are excluded by name. Similarly for animals which are cloven-hoofed but are not ruminant, the pig and the camel. Note that this failure to conform to the two necessary criteria for defining cattle is the only reason given in the Old Testament for avoiding the pig; nothing whatever is said about its dirty scavenging habits. As the pig does not yield milk, hide nor wool, there is no other reason for keeping it except for its flesh. And if the Israelites did not keep pig they would not be familiar with its habits. I suggest that originally the sole reason for its being counted as unclean is its failure as a wild boar to get into the antelope class, and that in this it is on the same footing as the camel and the hyrax, exactly as it is stated in the book.

After these borderline cases have been dismissed, the law goes on to deal with creatures according to how they live in the three elements, the water, the air and the earth. The principles here applied are rather different from those covering the camel, the pig, the hare and the hyrax. For the latter are excepted from clean food in having one but not both of the defining characters of livestock. Birds I can say nothing about, because, as I have said, they are named and not described and the translation of the name is open to doubt. But in general the underlying principle of cleanness in animals is that they shall conform fully to their class. Those species are unclean which are imperfect members of their class, or whose class itself confounds the general scheme of the world.

How does Douglas's explanation of the dietary laws change how you think about the passages from Deuteronomy and Leviticus?

**2.** In this chapter, I mention that the Apostle Peter had a vision in the Book of Acts that changed how the early followers of Jesus began to interact with the Old Testament dietary laws: "About noon the next day, as they were on their journey and approaching the city, Peter went up on the roof to pray. He became hungry and wanted something to eat; and while it was being prepared, he fell into a trance. He saw the heaven opened and something like a large sheet coming down, being lowered to the ground by its four corners. In it were all kinds of four-footed creatures and reptiles and birds of the air. Then he heard a voice saying, 'Get up, Peter; kill and eat.' But Peter said, 'By no means, Lord; for I have never eaten anything that is profane or unclean.' The voice said to him again, a second time, 'What God has made clean, you must not call profane.' This happened three times, and the thing was suddenly taken up to heaven." The next verse states that ". . . Peter was greatly puzzled about what to make of the vision that he had seen" (verse 17). In light of the passages from Leviticus and Deuteronomy, try to put yourself in Peter's shoes. What might he have pondered in those moments after experiencing the heavenly vision?

The Tanya, a Hasidic text, includes the following—how would you put this passage in conversation with Acts' account of what Peter heard? "Suppose you are tired and eat to regain the strength to perform a spiritual deed. If the food you eat is permitted, the act of eating elevates the food by using its energy in godly service. But if you unwittingly eat a forbidden food, even the intention of eating the food cannot elevate the food because the forbidden is held captive to the other side. What is true regarding what goes into your mouth is true regarding comes out as well. If you engage in innocent chatter meaning no harm, but wasting precious breath on the inconsequential, you can be cleansed. But if your speech is deliberately wicked, if you engage in mockery or slander, such deeds drag you into hell."

# THREE

# Avelut

### Mourning

Church funerals, when they tell the truth, not only remember lovingly the lives of the departed, they also preach the gospel—they proclaim that Jesus is risen, and insist that those who died in Him shall be risen too.

What churches often do less well is grieve. We lack a ritual for the long and tiring process that is sorrow and loss. A friend of mine whose husband recently died put it like this: "For about two weeks the church was really the church—really awesomely, wonderfully the church. Everyone came to the house, baked casseroles, carried Kleenex. But then the two weeks ended, and so did the consolation calls." While you the mourner are still bawling your eyes out and slamming fists into the wall, everyone else, understandably, forgets and goes back to their normal lives and you find, after all those crowds of people, that you are left alone. You are without the church, and without a church vocabulary for what happens to the living after the dead are dead.

Mourning, maybe, is never easy, but it is better done inside a communal grammar of bereavement. Christianity has a hopeful and true vocabulary for death-and-resurrection. It is Judaism that offers the grammar for in between, for the mourning after death and before Easter.

**CONSIDER CAREFULLY THE MOURNER'S *KADDISH*,**
the prayer that mourners say twice daily for a year after a death
in their family. Jews typically say it in Hebrew (whether or not they
generally read or speak the language) but here it is in English:

> Glorified and sanctified be God's great name
>> throughout the world
> which He has created according to His will.
> May He establish His kingdom in your lifetime and
>> during your days,
> and within the life of the entire House of Israel, speedily
>> and soon;
> and say, Amen.
> May His great name be blessed forever and to all
>> eternity.
> Blessed and praised, glorified and exalted, extolled and
>> honored,
> adored and lauded be the name of the Holy One,
>> blessed be He,
> beyond all the blessings and hymns, praises and
>> consolations that
> are ever spoken in the world; and say, Amen.
> May there be abundant peace from heaven, and life, for us
> and for all Israel; and say, Amen.
> He who creates peace in His celestial heights,
> may He create peace for us and for all Israel;
> and say, Amen.

What does this prayer say about mourning? What might
be the rationale for, or the fruit of, saying a prayer of praise
twice a day during bereavement?

∽

Judaism understands mourning as a discipline, one in which the mourner is not only allowed, but expected, to be engaged. Rather than asking the mourner to paper over his grief, the Jewish community supports him in mourning. (My priest, who is always urging me to pray the despairing Book of Psalms, says that Judaism mourns well in part because Jews understand lament. "Christians," he says, "do not know how to lament.")

Jewish bereavement marks the days, and then the months, and then all the years after a death. The first space, called *aninut* (literally "burial"), comprises the days after death and before burial. During these days, mourners are exempt from the other requirements of Jewish law—they are not obligated to attend prayer services or visit the sick or welcome guests, because they are devoted entirely to the one commandment of preparing the dead for a funeral, and that preparation is all-consuming. Rabbi Margaret Holub says that mourners are exempt from other commandments during *aninut* because only the living are

**IN MY CHURCH**, the Episcopal Church, we have the custom of saying, as we walk a casket or urn to the place it will be interred, "All of us go down to the dust; yet even at the grave we make our song: Alleluia, alleluia, alleluia." Though I have now said these words at countless funerals, it never fails to startle me. I find it beautiful and odd. Why do we sing alleluias as we go down to the grave?

obligated by God's law, and in those first days after a death, mourners "border on death themselves." Even the community has different obligations during the period of *aninut*: The community is not obligated to visit or comfort or feed the mourners, explains Rabbi Holub, because until the burial, "'the death is still happening,' so the work of comforting cannot yet begin."

Then the counting starts. The next demarked days are *shiva*, or "seven," the first week after burial. In that first week, mourners "sit *shiva*." The expression to sit *shiva* is enacted literally—after the funeral, you return home to sit on low chairs, as Job's friends did; "they sat down with him toward the ground for seven days and seven nights, and no one spoke a word to him." All the mirrors are draped in black, and the mourner lights a memorial candle, and she does not wash her hair or wear perfume or put on lipstick. Mourners do not have sex, or listen to music, or wear shoes. They do not leave the house the whole seven days, except on Shabbat. Their neighbors bring food. At the first meal after the funeral—called the *seudat havra'ah*, or the meal of recovery—the mourner is meant to eat an egg, whose obvious circular fertility is to begin the slow work of reminding the bereaved that she will live.

The next unit of mourning time is *shloshim*, thirty, the first month after death. Drawn, like *shiva*, from Scripture—the captive woman in Deuteronomy weeps for her parents for thirty days—*shloshim* also makes emotional sense. It is the edging back to worldly concerns and quotidian rhythms after the intense cocoon of *shiva*. During *shloshim*, the mourner may return to waiting tables or taking depositions or folding laundry or prowling the farmers' market. But she avoids large parties and celebrations and musical performances, attends no weddings except for those of the very closest relatives.

The Talmud divides this mourning month into four discrete weeks, marked by their respective Sabbaths. On the first Sabbath, mourners attend synagogue but wait outside during the celebratory songs that welcome the Sabbath bride. (As they reenter for the remainder of the service, the congregation proclaims, "May God console you among the other mourners of Zion and Jerusalem.") On the second Shabbat, mourners participate in the whole of the service, even the joyful Sabbath hymns, but they do not sit in their usual seat, "as if to indicate," in anthropologist Samuel Heilman's words, "that even on the Sabbath, with its respite from pain, they remain somehow communally unsettled." On the third Sabbath of *shloshim*, mourners return to their regular spot in the pews, but slip out of *shul* as soon as the service ends, avoiding neighborly chit-chat. Only on the fourth Sabbath of *shloshim* do mourners become, in the Talmud's phrase, "like all people," fully participating in the Shabbat of the community.

After this thirty days comes the full year of mourning, a period designated especially for those who mourn their parents. The central commandment of mourning is to say *Kaddish*, a short prayer that begins: "Magnified and sanctified may God's great name be." It is a prayer, actually, that appears at several places in the daily liturgy—once, twice, and then a special time again, the so-called mourner's *Kaddish*. It is one of the prayers that requires a quorum of ten adults—you are not allowed to say *Kaddish* alone in your house; rather, you are permitted to recite it only with the community of believers. The mourner is obligated to say this prayer twice a day, every day, for one full year of mourning. During *shiva*, the mourner must not leave his house to go to synagogue, and so the synagogue comes to him, daily

**AMY-JILL LEVINE**, a Jewish scholar of the New Testament, notes that there is a similarity between the *kaddish* and the Lord's Prayer: the second line of Matthew's Lord's Prayer, "'Hallowed be thy name' is," Levine writes, "a component of most Jewish prayers. . . . The Kaddish . . . begins, 'Magnified and sanctified be [God's] great name.'" Levine goes on to link many other phrases from the Lord's Prayer to ancient Jewish prayers. What is your response to the idea that there is a connection between the Lord's Prayer and Jewish prayers, including the *kaddish*?

services in a living room or kitchen or den. After *shiva*, he returns to the synagogue, and there, twice a day for a year, he says *Kaddish* for his parent.

*Yahrtzeit*—literally, in Yiddish, the time of one year—marks the anniversary of the death. Every year, on that anniversary, the mourner lights a special memorial candle, and once again stands in synagogue to say the mourner's *Kaddish*. Some people fast. Some people give a special donation in memory of their beloved. Others visit gravesides or study a chapter of Torah in honor of their dead. Still others take the day to look over old photographs, to raise a glass of whiskey in memory of, to recite psalms for the soul of—all different pieces of commemorating, remembering, celebrating, and mourning.

This calendar of bereavement recognizes the slow way that mourning works, the long time it takes a grave to cool, slower and longer than our zip-zoom Internet-and-fast-food society can easily accommodate. Long after your friends and

**JOHN 11:1–44** recounts a time of mourning in Jesus' life—this is the famous story of Jesus' realizing that Lazarus had died. Take some time to read the full passage of John 11:1–44. What do you make of Jesus' refusal to go to Lazarus while he was still alive? Why do you think Jesus wept?

Note that we hear the phrase "Come and see" in this story. This is not the first time we hear that phrase in the Gospel of John. It is actually the fourth, and final time. The first time happens way back in chapter 1, when Jesus first meets his disciples and they ask him where he is going. He says, "Come and see." It is an invitation—to follow Jesus and see what God is up to and see about the kind of things *we* might get up to as friends of Jesus. "Come and see," Jesus says to those first disciples—come and see what it means to be God's friend, and God's companion. And then we hear the phrase three more times, but never again from Jesus himself. We hear it instead from Jesus' followers, who are inviting *their* friends and acquaintances to come and see what life with God is like. Phillip, wanting to introduce his friend Nathaniel to Jesus, tells Nathaniel all about Jesus and then says, "Come and see." A little while later, a Samarian woman who has had a long conversation with Jesus at a well outside of town runs back to her town square and tells all her neighbors "I think I have just met the messiah. Come and see!" Come and see this new teacher and healer! Come and see where life as his friend might lead. And then this fourth and final iteration. This time, it is Mary who utters our phrase, but she's not speaking to a coworker or kinswoman who hasn't yet met Jesus. She is speaking to Jesus himself. "Where is your brother?", Jesus asks her. "Come and see," she says. It sounds rather different when she says it. *Come and see where life as your friend leads. It leads to this. It leads to death.* And that is when Jesus weeps. Perhaps he weeps because he is overcome by Mary's own weeping. Perhaps he weeps because he suddenly regrets not having come to Lazarus sooner. And perhaps he weeps because Mary has just shown him something of his own future. He weeps because he has been brought face to face with the strong reality of death.

Jesus' weeping at the tomb is not the only instance of God's tears. In Jeremiah, a text written to and about the exile of Israel, God weeps:

> For the wound of the daughter of my people is my heart
> wounded;
> I mourn, and dismay has taken hold on me.
> Is there no balm in Gilead?
> Is there no physician there?
> Why then has the health of the daughter of my people
> not been restored?
> Oh that my head were waters,
> and my eyes a fountain of tears,
> that I might weep day and night
> for the slain of the daughter of my people!
> [Jer. 8:21–9:1 ESV]

How is God's weeping an expression of God's solidarity with suffering people? Does the image of God's erupting in tears startle you? Disturb you? Console you?

acquaintances have stopped paying attention, after they have forgotten to ask how you are and pray for you and hold your hand, you are still in a place of ebbing sadness. Mourning plateaus gradually, and the diminishing of intensity is both recognized and nurtured by the different spaces the Jewish mourning rituals create—the harrowing shock of *aninut*, the pain of *shiva*, the stepping into life and world of *shloshim*. (The rabbis would be quick to point out that we do not observe the calendar of mourning because it is psychologically beneficial, but because it is commanded—and that is true, but why should it be surprising that God commanded something that therapists might now applaud?)

∾

Whenever I have paid a *shiva* call (the idiom may recall Emily Post, but it's just the term used to describe the communal obligation to turn up at a mourner's home and murmur comforting words), what has always struck me is the sheer crush of people. People in the den, people in the kitchen, people crowding out on the terrace and pressed into the hallway. The mourner who wants to weep in his cups alone is out of luck. On those days when he desires nothing more than to crawl back under the covers and shut out everything that breathes and has three dimensions, people pack into his home. On the last day of *shiva*, friends come and escort him, holding his arm or inching along his side, out the driveway and down the street and around the block, a symbolic (but not merely symbolic) reentry into society. Then twice a day for a year, he is forbidden to pray alone and commanded to pray with people, showing up at synagogue to do right by his dead and say *Kaddish* for them, not alone in his den but there in the community of God's faithful.

Not only is the community present for one's mourning, God is present too. God is ubiquitous in Jewish bereavement because of the *Kaddish*. Countless commentators have observed that the *Kaddish* is a curious mourner's prayer, because it says nothing about mourning. It is rather a prayer about God, describing Him as magnified and sanctified and worthy to be praised. It is not a prayer of rent garments and commemoration, but rather simply four verses of praise to God. "Blessed, praised, glorified, exalted, extolled, mighty, upraised, and lauded be the Name of the Holy One, Blessed is He, beyond any blessing or song." As one mourner noted, the *Kaddish* is really "a Gloria." Even in the pit, even in depression and loss and nonsense, still we respond

**THE TALMUD TELLS US** that "when God remembered the suffering of God's children in exile, God dropped two tears into the ocean. The sound of these tears, heard from one end of the earth to the other, had a seismological effect, causing tremors to shake the earth." Jewish theologian Herbert Basser says that from this Talmudic tale, we learn that "God's love of Israel shines through his tears. The rabbis find nothing more powerful than the immensity of these tears and note their chaotic potential: the vibrations can lead to earthquakes and seismic tremors. God's tears, though controlled, and but two in number, can wreak havoc." How might God's tears have power today?

to God with praise. This is not to say that the mourner should not feel what he feels—anger, disbelief, hatred. He can feel those things (and shout them out to God; God can take it). You do not have to feel praise in the intense moments of mourning, but the praise is still true, and insisting upon it over and over, twice a day every day, ensures that eventually you will come to remember the truth of those praises.

I am still both young and lucky. My parents are alive, and my sister, and all my aunts and uncles and cousins, and even

**AS AN EPISCOPAL PRIEST,** I am guided by the Book of Common Prayer when I officiate at a funeral. My favorite prayer from the funeral service—indeed, one of my favorite prayers ever—is this:

> Into your hands, O merciful Savior, we commend your servant *N.* Acknowledge, we humbly beseech you, a sheep of your own fold, a lamb of your own flock, a sinner of your own redeeming. Receive him into the arms of your mercy, into the blessed rest of everlasting peace, and into the glorious company of the saints in light. *Amen.*

> How might it feel to pray this prayer when someone you love dies? What might it mean to think of yourself as a sheep of God's own fold, a lamb of God's own flock, a sinner of God's own redeeming?

one grandparent. I can still number in the single digits the funerals I've attended, and only one of them really mattered to me, the funeral of my nearest and dearest in England, just shortly after I became a Christian. Her name was Clementine (as in the fruit, or the lost-and-gone-forever Valentine song), and she was driving on those swirling roads outside of Oxford and was killed by someone who later admitted to drinking seven or eight highballs before he got into his car.

It was sudden, of course, and horrible, and Clementine's friends and family and all the people who loved her bricolaged their way into grief. We prayed the rite for the dead. We held an all-night vigil. We sent checks to Mothers Against Drunk Driving. We sang her favorite hymns, and wore the sweaters she had loaned us and not yet reclaimed. And we put our pictures of her in picture frames, and were sad.

I described all this in an e-mail to my friend Shelby in New York. "Like all mourners," I wrote, "none of us who mourn Clementine really know what to do. It is all so shocking and unexpected and ridiculous and awful." Shelby reminded me that I might not know what to do in the face of this death, but the tradition that raised me knew what to do. "You could say *Kaddish*," she wrote.

I was not blood or marriage kin to Clementine, so, according to the particulars of Jewish law, even had I still been a practicing Jew, I was not a mourner, one who would sit on a low stool or say *Kaddish*. But my e-mail interlocutor had reminded me of the rhythm of mourning. I found, in the weeks after Clementine's death, that I did not want to listen to music, that I could not, in fact, tolerate celebration of any kind. I even found it faintly annoying when a passerby whistled or hummed. Then, perhaps three months after Clementine died, some voice in my head told me that I was overdue, that I had been sitting sackcloth for far longer than the thirty days of *shloshim*. So that night I went to hear the choir performing at St. John's College. I thought of Clementine at this concert (not something lofty like "she would have loved this ethereal music," but rather that she would have trashed the bouffant hair and vinyl fingernails of the woman sitting directly to my left).

I have not said *Kaddish*.

On the anniversary of her death, I will send another check to MADD.

I have purchased a *yahrtzeit* candle and closeted it away in my linen closet, and on October 19 I will pull it out and find some matches and remember my dead.

# Discussion Questions

**1.** In this chapter, I discuss the practices that Jewish mourners follow to help them move from the initial shock of death and gradually, back into community life. What is your initial response to the Jewish mourning process? Consider the painful deaths you have experienced. Do you think any of these practices—sitting *shiva*, the month of *shloshim*, or the year of saying daily prayers—would have helped you in your own mourning process? Why or why not?

**2.** The Jewish tradition of mourning is a community endeavor just as much as it is a personal process. When the mourner sits *shiva*, neighbors and community members bring food to him daily, and at the end of the week, "friends come and escort him, holding his arm or inching along his side, out the driveway and down the street and around the block, a symbolic (but not merely symbolic) reentry into society" (page 46). Leon Wieseltier, who wrote a moving and learned memoir about his experience saying *kaddish* for his father, notes that "When you mourn for your father, you serve things larger than him. Mourning is mandated by more than its object and by more than its occasion. It is mandated by one's location in a family, in a tradition, in a world." How do the Jewish practices outlined in this chapter help both the individual mourner *and* the larger religious community that surrounds the mourner? What does the mourner learn in the process? What do the community members learn?

**3.** Judaism offers mourners a calendar of mourning (a choreographed year of mourning) and ways for the community to be drawn into an individual's bereavement (the mourner can only say the mourner's *kaddish* with other people). Are there ways we can do those two things, calendar and community, in the local church? Do Christian communities have any rites of mourning that engage both the mourner and the larger church? How do these traditions—if they exist—help the individual and the community? Or, what is lacking in the

Christian tradition that can be informed—and helped—by the Jewish tradition?

**4.** According to historian Derek Krueger, in the fourth century, John Chrysostom attacked "funeral customs [that] focused on 'excessive' mourning. [Chrysostom] viewed highly emotional displays of grief as a pagan tendency and an implicit denial of the truth of the Resurrection. After the coming of Christianity, true believers had no reason to be upset by death. Instead, Christians were to mourn living sinners, because although worms were not yet eating their bodies, their passions were shredding their souls to pieces. . . . After the death of a loved one, men should not beat themselves and should not invite pagan women to sing dirges at funerals. On the other hand, inviting poor people to funerals and priests to pray in order to help the souls of the dead was, in Chrysostom's view, consistent with Christian teachings about death, so long as this was done with the proper acknowledgment that sin was the problem, not death." Do you agree with Chrysostom that "true believers [have] no reason to be upset by death"? Is it possible to mourn too much?

**5.** In this chapter, I write that "Christian funerals, when they tell the truth, not only remember lovingly the lives of the departed, they also preach the gospel—they proclaim that Jesus is risen, and insist that those who died in Him shall be risen too" (page 38). Consider that alongside of Chrysostom's statement above regarding "excessive mourning." How does a Christian mourn and proclaim the resurrection at the same time? Are the two things mutually exclusive? Do you think today's practices make likely too much mourning or too little?

6. Canadian writer Katherine Ashenburg tells this story about the longing people today feel for mourning rituals (in this case, mourning garb): "Matthew Galleli is a teacher in Rochester. About a month after his wife died . . . wanting to counteract the assumption that his grieving was finished, he began wearing a black ribbon and a white ribbon looped together on his lapel. He chose ribbons because they have been used to raise awareness of issues [such as AIDS and breast cancer], and when people asked him about them, he told them he was mourning his wife. . . . As Galleli said, his ribbons were 'a way to let folks know that something different has happened.' That sounds modest enough, but mourners will tell you there are days when it is crucially important. Mourning clothes provided a marker and thus a kind of insulation for those who wore them—rare luxuries now that we have nothing that alerts the community to the presence of a mourner." How did Matthew Galleli's ribbons engage both calendar and community? What other mourning practices can you imagine adopting, or encouraging your church community to adopt?

# FOUR

# Hachnassat orchim

### Hospitality

F ew situations make me as uncomfortable as being a new-comer in a church where I know nothing and no one. Everyone else knows when to stand and sit and bow and smile, and everyone else has someone to talk to during coffee hour, and there I stand, awkward and ill at ease, my inner introvert yelling at me to go home and curl up with a novel. (This can be especially torturous at Episcopal churches, which insist upon the theologically sound but socially hideous ritual of "passing the peace." Right after the Prayers of the People and right before the announcements, the Episcopal worshiper is required to turn to a neighbor, shake a hand, and say, "May the peace of the Lord be with you." If you know your fellow worshipers, this is a nice chatting break in the middle of the service. If you do not, you feel like a loser.)

That was how it was my second Sunday in Charlottesville. I was at Christ Church, where I knew exactly two people. (One of them was my mother, and what single woman wants to get stuck at coffee hour eating donut holes with her mom?) After the service ended, I managed to silence my introvert long enough to introduce myself to a couple sitting in the pew behind me.

"Hi," they said. "So pleased to meet you." I complimented the wife's shoes, the husband asked if I'd enjoyed the sermon, and then they said, "If you don't have plans for the Fourth of July, please come to our party."

This unexpected July Fourth invitation struck me as exceptional, even though I was back in the friendly South. In the coming weeks, though, I came to see that in the Charlottesville Christian community, opening one's home seems to be *de rigueur*. To wit, the experience of my friend Suzanne: Suzanne found herself with a gap between leases, and within two days she'd had three offers of spare bedrooms from fellow parishioners.

Or consider my friends the Hanovers: So often do the Hanovers have guests for dinner that when they are guestless, eight-year-old Julianne asks, "Mommy, why is no one in the guest chair tonight?"

Or this, my favorite example of Charlottesville hospitality: One evening I attended a training session for Lay Eucharistic Ministers, those non-ordained folk who hold the chalice to your lips when you come to the altar to receive Communion. There were maybe nine of us at this meeting, and only two were this side of fifty—me, and a tall blonde man with a Georgia accent and the improbable name of Griff Gatewood (makes him sound like he's an Anne Rivers Siddons character, but he's really a real, live person). At the end of the meeting, Griff Gatewood came up to me and said, "Do you have community here with people your own age?" That is exactly what he said, verbatim. And then he invited me to have homemade pizza with him and some friends that very night. (The true confession slice of this vignette is that now the tall blonde man is my boyfriend, but that boyfriendness did not happen for months and months, so I

**"IT IS RELATED OF R. JOSHUA** that he extended hospitality [to all]. A man arrived to whom he gave food and drink, took up to the attic and then removed the ladder from under him. What did the man do? He arose in the middle of the night, spread out his cloak, took the vessels [belonging to the room] which he wrapped in his cloak and was about to descend when he fell and broke his collar-bone. In the morning R. Joshua came and, finding him [on the ground], said to him, 'You worthless person, do men act like you?' He replied, 'I did not know that you had removed the ladder from under me'. He said to him, 'Were you not aware that we were on our guard against you since yesterday?'" This story relates how one of the ancient rabbis, R. Joshua, invited a man into his home, while at the same time protecting himself from the possibility of being robbed by removing the ladder from under the attic where the visitor was sleeping. The man did, in fact, try to steal from him, but was found out because he fell and broke his collarbone, not knowing that the ladder had been taken away. Is it possible to offer hospitality to others while still being "on your guard" against them? Should we balance hospitality with a sort of worldly wisdom?

Offering hospitality to others—strangers or friends—opens us up to new levels of vulnerability and even to the possibility of being taken advantage of. What worries you when you think about offering hospitality?

stand by my vignette as an example of hospitality, not flirtation. He is, in fact, one of the most intentionally hospitable people I know, which is one of the many reasons I am pleased the boyfriendness happened eventually.)

After a year in Charlottesville, I have grown so accustomed to the ubiquitous hospitality that I almost don't notice it anymore. But it is noteworthy, because it is part of what the church is supposed to be: a community of people practicing hospitality.

Hospitality is not, of course, unique to Charlottesville. I first learned what real hospitality looked like from the Orthodox Jewish community in New York. In my case, what it looked like was moving to Manhattan at age sixteen and being embraced by a few families who knew little about me other that that I was new, my family was far away, and I needed somewhere to eat lunch on Shabbat. I was never without an invitation for Sabbath or holiday meals. The Farmer family, in particular, held me to an open-door policy—turn up, sleep, eat, talk, shower, hang out, anytime, no need to phone ahead.

In Hebrew, this is *hachnassat orchim*, literally "the bringing in of guests." Sociologists might suggest that Jews do hospitality so well because they have spent so many centuries being the stranger and the friendless. It is also true that Jewish (and so also Christian) sacred Scripture is thick with the practice of hospitality. More than once, God instructs His people to welcome the stranger because "you were strangers in the land of Egypt." And there is story after story of Hebrews and Gentiles alike doing just that. Abraham gives food to three strangers who turn out to be angels come to announce Isaac's birth (it is this to which the Epistle to the Hebrews refers when it instructs, "Do not be forgetful to entertain strangers; for thereby some have entertained angels unawares"). In the Book of Exodus, Jethro was eager to welcome Moses when he sojourned through Midian. Rahab, a prostitute, was blessed for giving shelter to Joshua's spies. In 2 Kings, we read of a nameless Shunammite woman who welcomes the prophet Elisha into her home.

Later rabbinic literature surrounds the biblical stories and models with codes and instructions. Rabbi Yochanan insisted that practicing hospitality was even more important than praying. Some rabbis turn hospitality into architecture, urging faithful Jews to build houses with doors on all four sides so that travelers and guests might find a welcome door from any direction. Many Jewish communities adopted the idea of serving all their dinner courses at once; this way finicky guests would not have to suffer through an appetizer or bowl of soup they did not like.

Early Christian communities continued these practices of hospitality, attempting to feed the poor, host travelers, visit the imprisoned, invite widows and orphans to join them at mealtime—all expressions of a capacious notion of hospitality. A second-century Christian text known as the Didache instructed Jesus' followers to help visiting travelers "all you can." In a sermon on Acts, renowned fourth-century preacher John Chrysostom told heads of house not merely to delegate hospitality to their servants but to "personally welcome those [strangers and guests] who come" to your home. In the sixth century, Julianus Pomerius (sounding a little like Rabbi Yochanan) insisted that hospitality took precedence over other spiritual disciplines: He enjoined his readers to break a fast and "unbend one's self" in order to share a meal with others.

**THE RISK OF HOSPITALITY NOTWITHSTANDING**, the writer of Hebrews encourages us to show gratuitous hospitality: "Let mutual love continue. Do not neglect to show hospitality to strangers, for by doing that some have entertained angels without knowing it." As I mention earlier in this chapter, the author of Hebrews is referring to the story in Genesis 18 in which Abraham welcomed three strangers and fed them; these strangers were actually the angels of the Lord. John Chrysostom, to whom we turned in the last chapter, continues this line of thought: "If others have plundered your property, display your hospitality out of such things as you have. What excuse, then, shall we have, when they even after the spoiling of their goods, were thus admonished? And he did not say, 'Do not neglect' to entertain strangers, but 'to show hospitality'; that is, do not merely entertain strangers, but do it with love for the strangers. Moreover, he did not speak of the recompense that is future and in store for us, lest he should make them more supine, but of that already given. For 'thereby some,' he says, 'have entertained angels unawares.'" Chrysostom says that there is a present reward given for showing hospitality to the stranger, the outsider, even if we have already been "plundered." What types of rewards do you potentially see in offering hospitality to others? Have you experienced any unexpected rewards when you have extended hospitality?

The Apostle Paul placed such a high value on hospitality that he listed it—along with temperance, sobriety, and gentleness— among the characteristics required of leaders of the church.

❧

Christians and Jews hold in common one theological basis for hospitality: Creation. Creation is the ultimate expression of God's hospitality to His creatures. In the words of one rabbi, everything God created is a "manifestation of His kindness. [The] world is one big hospitality inn." As church historian Amy Oden has put it, "God offers hospitality to all humanity . . . by establishing a home . . . for all." To invite people into

**JUST AS GOD CREATED THE WORLD** and offered it as a home for all humankind, we are to mirror God's hospitality to others by opening our homes to them. Origen, a third-century Christian theologian, takes this idea of hospitality past our own front doors: "We must not look on the saints as beggars but see them as people who have needs like our own. The practice of hospitality does not simply mean that we should entertain those who come to us. It means also that we should go out and invite others to come in." How can you practically "go out and invite others to come in" during this next week? What things might you have to give up—practically or emotionally—to participate in tangible hospitality to neighbors or strangers?

our homes is to respond with gratitude to the God who made a home for us.

In the Christian doctrine of the Trinity, we find another resource for hospitality. The Trinity shows God in relationship with Himself. Our Three-in-One God has welcomed us into Himself and invited us to participate in divine life. And so the invitation that we as Christians extend to one another is not simply an invitation into our homes or to our tables; what we ask of other people is that they enter into our lives.

Some Christians have embraced hospitality with vigorous radicalism. All across the world, at places like L'Arche and the Catholic Worker houses, communities have oriented their lives toward hospitality, serving the poor and, in the most literal way, inviting strangers off the streets and into their homes.

Is, then, the Charlottesville model a bourgeois cop-out? Easy, ersatz hospitality that looks lame when held up against the hard work of all those Catholic Workers? I'm willing to entertain those arguments—and willing to cede that my friend John, who lives with and breaks bread with the working poor and unemployed in Charlottesville's housing projects, is probably earning special crowns in heaven. But the church fathers' instructions about the poor and strangers can encompass even our neighbors in the suburbs. To throw a dinner party is not to abandon the poor; it is to begin hospitality with people you know.

Not only am I a far cry from Dorothy Day, I am not even very good at luncheon hospitality. I want to be. I try to be. But I am too busy, my kitchen is too small, inviting people over takes too much time, my apartment is always too messy.

But in that list of excuses is a set of pointers about what hospitality is and is not, what it does and does not require. It does require a bit of intentionality. My lease is up next month, and I have decided to move. Among the reasons to move is space. I don't need a bigger apartment, but I need an apartment where the space is configured differently. A tour of my home will show you why. I have a huge office, and in that office sits a wonderful old picnic table, and on the picnic table sits my computer. I have a tiny kitchen, and against the kitchen wall is a writing desk that used to live in a college library. My apartment is, in other words, a great place to work, but a lousy place to eat or entertain. I almost never invite people over for dinner—their options would be to eat on the floor or eat at my desk. My new apartment, I hope, will have a smaller office and a larger kitchen, and maybe the table will fit in the room where people eat, and the writing desk in the room where people write. In other words, I have realized that I want to create a home in which friends are welcome, and my current home simply is not that. So I'm moving. (Meanwhile, if you drop by for a piece of pizza, I will crouch with you on the floor.)

Intentionality, however, is not perfection. Let's consider that very last excuse in my list, the seemingly innocent insistence that my apartment is never tidy enough for guests. Well, now. I probably shouldn't have curdling milk in the fridge if I'm inviting someone over for tea, and it might be nice if I emptied the kitchen trash can and didn't leave dirty clothes all over the bathroom floor. But to be a hostess, I'm going to have to surrender my notions of *Good Housekeeping* domestic perfection. I will have to set down my pride and invite people over even if I have not dusted. This is tough: My mother set a high standard. Her house is always immaculate, most especially if she's expecting company. But if I wait for immaculate, I will never have a guest.

God's Creation gives us a model for making and sharing homes with people, but the reality of God's Trinitarian life suggests that Christian hospitality goes further than that. We are not meant simply to invite people into our homes, but also to invite them into our lives. Having guests and visitors, if we do it right, is not an imposition, because we are not meant to rearrange our lives for our guests—we are meant to invite our guests to enter into our lives as they are. It is this forging of relationships that transforms entertaining (i.e., deadly dull cocktail parties at the country club) into hospitality (i.e., a simple pizza on my floor). As writer Karen Burton Mains puts it, "Visitors may be more than guests in our home. If they like, they may be friends."

I don't find inviting people into my life  much easier than inviting them into my apartment. At its core, I think, cultivating an intimacy in which people can know and be known requires being honest—practicing that other Christian discipline of tell-ing the truth about where we live and how we got there. Often, I'd rather dissemble. Often, just as I'd rather welcome guests into a cozy and cute apartment worthy of *Southern Living,* I'd rather show them a Lauren who is perfect and put-together and serene. Often, telling the truth feels absurd.

Not too long ago, Griff and I were at a New Year's party, attended, it seemed, by just about everyone we knew. People were sipping mulled cider and playing charades and discussing resolutions and the new leaves they would turn over, and at one point, a curvy red-headed twenty-year-old, who happened to have known Griff for a million years and who happened also to be my student, threw herself off the dance floor and into Griff's arms, for an entirely innocent, and very twenty-year-old appropriate, New Year's hug.

The next week I was chatting about some school matter with the redhead (let's call her Rita Hayworth). I was in mature, collected, professional mode—my hair was even in a chignon—and was not expecting Rita to ask, sweetly, if I had felt uncomfortable about The Hug. I wanted to sound like a grown-up. I wanted to blandly laugh and say, "No, not at all, don't be ridiculous." But some instinct told me to risk transparency with Rita H., that if I couldn't tell her the faintly lame and faintly embarrassing truth about my silly, sad emotions, how was I ever going to be able to tell the truth about something big? So I tried. I told her that actually, when she took that flying dance floor leap into Griff, I felt old and uncool and insecure, and also wondered all sorts of things about boundaries and friendship, and had wanted to kill them both. This truth-telling, to be sure, didn't change the world; but it did push me and Rita a bit closer to real knowledge of one another.

Standing there with Rita Hayworth, I understood why Julianus Pomerius had spoken of hospitality as unbending one's self. In this unbending there was a genuine return to *hachnassat orchim*, to an inviting of guests. The irony is that the unbending requires inviting my neighbors into the very places where I am most bent.

So you see that asking people into my life is not so different from asking them into my apartment. Like my apartment, my interior life is never going to be wholly respectable, cleaned up, and gleaming. But that is where I live. In the certitude of God, I ought to be able to risk issuing the occasional invitation.

# Discussion Questions

**1.** In this chapter, I discuss that the tradition of extending hospitality and opening one's home to a guest or wayfarer is both an ancient Jewish and Christian tradition. Because the Israelites were often sojourners themselves, God's care for the foreigner is a common theme in the Hebrew Bible. For example, Leviticus 19:34: "The alien who resides with you shall be to you as the citizen among you; you shall love the alien as yourself, for you were aliens in the land of Egypt: I am the LORD your God."

What do we learn about God's character from this passage? What does it mean for us to worship, and be created, by a God who cares for the "alien"?

I often think about this passage from Leviticus when I read a newspaper article about immigration reform.

Christian theologian Luke Bretherton reads Leviticus 19:34 to mean "true hospitality requires we both understand the experience of being a vulnerable stranger and what it means to receive all things from God?" Do you feel that you understand either of these, let alone both? For middle-class Americans, it can be especially hard to "understand the experience of being a vulnerable stranger."

**2.** I mention the story of the "nameless Shunammite woman" in the book of 2 Kings who offers hospitality to Elisha, a prophet:

> One day Elisha was passing through Shunem, where a wealthy woman lived, who urged him to have a meal. So whenever he passed that way, he would stop there for a meal. She said to her husband, "Look, I am sure that this man who regularly passes our way is a holy man of God. Let us make a small roof chamber with walls, and put there for him a bed, a table, a chair, and a lamp, so that he can stay there whenever he comes to us." One day when he came there, he went up to the chamber and lay down there. He said to his servant Gehazi, "Call the Shunammite woman." When he had called her, she stood before him. He said to him, "Say to her, Since you have taken all this trouble for us, what may be done for you? Would you have a word spoken on your behalf to the king or to the commander of the army?" She answered, "I live among my own people." He said, "What then may be done for her?" Gehazi answered, "Well, she has no son, and her husband is old." He said, "Call her." When he had called her, she stood at the door. He said, "At this season, in due time, you shall embrace a son." She replied, "No, my lord, O man of God; do not deceive your servant." The woman conceived and bore a son at that season, in due time, as Elisha had declared to her. (2 Kings 4:8–17)

The Shunammite woman saw that Elisha was a frequent traveler in her area of Shunem. Not only did she welcome him into her home; she also provided a lodging place for him to use whenever he came by. Recently, when my marriage was foundering and I had to find a place to stay for a few months, my priest and her family took me in, giving me a twin bed in a small guest room. At first, this seemed like the height of patheticness—who winds up at 32 in someone's spare twin bed? But over the four months I was there, it came to seem like holy hospitality—as if my priest had indeed prepared a room for me just as the Shunammite woman had prepared a room for Elisha.

Are there any people in your life who would appreciate a similar "open door policy" if you offered it? Is your home a place where others can freely come and go? Why is it often difficult, in our culture, to have such openness with others?

**3.** The Gospel of Luke includes the famous story of Zacchaeus:

> He entered Jericho and was passing through it. A man was there named Zacchaeus; he was a chief tax collector and was rich. He was trying to see who Jesus was, but on account of the crowd he could not, because he was short in stature. So he ran ahead and climbed a sycamore tree to see him, because he was going to pass that way. When Jesus came to the place, he looked up and said to him, "Zacchaeus, hurry and come down; for I must stay at your house today." So he hurried down

and was happy to welcome him. All who saw it began to grumble and said, "He has gone to be the guest of one who is a sinner." Zacchaeus stood there and said to the Lord, "Look, half of my possessions, Lord, I will give to the poor; and if I have defrauded anyone of anything, I will pay back four times as much." (Luke 19:1–8)

What do you make of this remarkable story? Zacchaeus was utterly converted to justice and generosity by practicing hospitality—by hosting Jesus. And Jesus did not wait to be invited—He invited himself over! Has Jesus ever invited himself over to your house? Did it inspire you to generosity, and to make things right with people you might have harmed?

# FIVE

# Tefillah

## Prayer

My first, most formative prayer lessons came at the synagogue, in the person of Ruby Lichtenstein. I was thirteen when I met Ruby, who seemed impossibly old—I think she was in her mid-fifties, but she was an old mid-fifties. She was heavy-set. She dyed her hair a color that can only be called tangerine. And she wore pastel wool suits all the time, even in summer. Perhaps an unlikely prayer teacher, but one day, shortly before my Bat Mitzvah, she took me aside and gave me a talking-to.

"Lauren," she said, "you are going to get lots of presents in the next few weeks. You are going to get earrings and *kiddush* cups and books." (She was right. Among other goodies, I received thirteen silver bracelets, two evening bags, two *challah* covers, and a copy of *Changing Bodies, Changing Lives*, a guide to puberty put out by the Boston Women's Health Collective.) "I," said Ruby, "am going to give you your most important present." The present was wrapped in a plastic grocery bag. It was a *siddur*, a prayer book. "Lauren Winner," she said, "a mark of being a Jew is praying to your God. This book is the way that Jews pray."

Jewish prayer is essentially book prayer, liturgical prayer. Jews say the same set prayers, at the same fixed hours, over and over, every day. There is, to be sure, room for spontaneous prayer (think of Tevye's off-the-cuff conversations with God in *Fiddler on the Roof),* but those spontaneous prayers are to the liturgy what grace notes are to a musical score: They decorate, but never drown out, the central theme. In the words of Jewish liturgical scholar Lawrence Hoffman, "Jews do offer freely composed prayers. . . . But overall, it is the fixed order and content of Jewish prayer that gives it its distinctiveness and that demands the personal commitment to prayer as a discipline."

Judaism is not the only religion to pray liturgically. *Salah,* the five-times-a-day Muslim prayer, is also liturgical. The American Buddhist Congress is developing a Buddhist liturgy, urging a "flexible standardization of the liturgy so that anyone attending [a] service anywhere in the country could feel at home, understand, and join in." And many Christians—in particular, Anglicans, Catholics, and the Eastern Orthodox—rely on prayer books, reciting set prayers at set hours of each day.

There are, to be sure, many styles of prayer, and I have dabbled in them all: I have prayed a rosary; I have traveled to California to walk a labyrinth; sometimes, when I am taking a walk or lying in bed or washing dishes, I chat with God as though talking to Ginger or Griff or Molly about this and that and what I wish for or fear. (On very, very rare occasions this chatting happens in the presence of other people, a three-way conversation among me and a buddy and God. One such rare occasion was dinner last week with my friend Kay. It was warm out, and Kay was smiling, wearing short-shorts and a snazzy tank top. I was a mess, fingers tapping and eyes distracted and not much sleep, worried about an e-mail exchange I'd had with my dad and wondering if I would ever know how to be a half-way decent daughter. "Well," said Kay, "we're just going to talk to the Lord about that right now." And we did—out loud, there at our wrought-iron table on the patio of the Biltmore Grill, right in front of half of Charlottesville. I am still a little bit uncomfortable with this out-loud-in-plain-view-with-other-people-right-there kind of prayer, but I am trying to learn.)

These are all good pieces of prayer, and I am glad to have them. But the skeleton that gives all these various prayings shape is liturgical prayer—the set prayers that I read every day from my prayer book. On good days, I say these prayer-book prayers at three different intervals—morning, noon, and evening. (Some days, however, are not good days, and on those days I let my morning prayers carry me all the way through to midnight.) This prayer-book praying is the way I learned to pray as a Jew. Now, as a Christian, the prayers I say are different—they are made in the name of Jesus; they talk about the Holy Spirit; they often quote St. Paul. But much of the work of the liturgy is the same.

### RABBI AMMI SAID:

"A person's prayer is not acceptable unless one's heart is in one's hands."

What do you think Rabbi Ammi means? What would it mean for you, personally, to pray with your heart in your hands?

Jews, it seems, have been saying set prayers since biblical times. Scripture instructs Jews to recite the *Shema*—"Hear O Israel, the Lord your God, the Lord is One"—upon waking and upon retiring. Liturgical prayer became essential to Jewish practice during the sixth century BCE when Jews, in exile from Jerusalem, had no way to get to the Temple to perform their traditional sacrifices. Communities of exiled Jews met regularly on the Sabbath and holidays, but in lieu of Temple sacrifices, they offered God prayers. During the next century, Jewish elders composed the *Amidah*, or "the standing" (because one stands while reciting it). This prayer, made up of eighteen separate blessings, is recited three times a day. There is more to Jewish liturgy than the *Shema* and *Amidah*; there are hymns of praise and prayers of petition and psalms. The synagogue newcomer can feel overwhelmed, but you get the hang of it quickly—it doesn't take too many weeks of reciting a prayer thrice daily before you know it as well as you know your own phone number.

It's the phone number sort of knowledge that has given liturgy such a bad rap in some quarters. "It's boring!" wails my friend Meg, who opted out of the thoroughgoingly liturgical

---

**MANY VOICES IN JUDAISM AND CHRISTIANITY** encourage people to set aside certain times, and certain places, for prayer. "Be sure to fix for yourself a place for your prayer," says the Derech Hayim. The same text also suggests, "It is appropriate to have special clothes which you wear only for prayer." Perhaps putting on those clothes or going to that place will help you know that you are, indeed, going to prayer.

---

Episcopal Church after about six months. "I tuned out. Instead of expressing my innermost feelings to God I was just reciting a bunch of old prayers by rote."

Liturgy can be dull, and its dullness can be distracting. Sometimes I set aside time specifically for prayer: I turn off the ringer on my phone and light a candle and sit in my best praying chair (the club chair with the red checked slipcover; don't ask me why, but it's generally the best); and even then I can look down at the prayer book in my hands and realize that I've been reading aloud for ten minutes, yet I have no idea what I've said. My mouth may have been mouthing psalms, but my brain was thinking grocery lists or weekend plans.

But if roteness is a danger, it is also the way liturgy works. When you don't have to think all the time about what words you are going to say next, you are free to fully enter into the act of praying; you are free to participate in the life of God.

Put differently: I have sometimes set aside my prayer book for days and weeks on end, and I find, at the end of those days and weeks on end, that I have lapsed into narcissism. Though meaning to commune with or reverence or at least acknowledge God, I wind up talking to myself about my emotions *du jour*. I worry about my mother's health, or I stress about money, or (more happily) I bop up and down with excitement about good news or sunshine or life in general, but I never get much further than that. It is returning to my prayer book that places me: places me in words that ask me to confess my sins, even when I can't think of any red-letter deeds recently committed; words that ask me to pray for presidents and homeless Charlottesvillians and everyone in between; words that praise God even on the mornings when I wonder if God exists at all. (Of course, sometimes the liturgy grandly expresses just exactly what we feel. When you have had a lousy day at work and have used every curse word you can think of to describe your boss, try an imprecatory psalm, such as Psalm 35: "May those who seek my life be disgraced and put to shame; may those who plot my ruin be turned back in dismay. . . . May their path be dark and slippery, with the angel of the LORD pursuing them.")

What I say to Meg is this: Sure, sometimes it is great when, in prayer, we can express to God just what we feel; but better still when, in the act of praying, our feelings change. Liturgy is not, in the end, open to our emotional whims. It repoints the person praying, taking him somewhere else.

A few weeks ago, Griff and I went to Americus, Georgia. This was no run-of-the-mill trip. This was dating baptism-by-fire. During our thirty-six hours in Americus, I visited his high school, two Habitat for Humanity houses he'd helped build, and the clothing shop where he bought his first suit. I shook hands with his high school algebra teacher and his pastor (and, I'm sure, a few unidentified ex-girlfriends), and I met almost a dozen Gatewood relatives.

One of the relatives was Granddaddy Gatewood. Dr. Gatewood is, as we in the South say, in decline; and he has been declining, I gather, for the better part of a decade. He does not remember much. In the afternoon he did not remember having met me in the morning. He does not remember Griff's name, or that Anna is his granddaughter and pregnant, or the tune to "America the Beautiful," or how long it takes to get from home to church.

The Gatewoods filled an entire pew at church, and I sat near the end, between Griff and his grandfather, who sat on the end

**THINK THAT THE LETTERS OF PRAYER** are the garments of God. What a joy to be making a garment for the greatest of kings! Enter into every letter with all your strength. God dwells within each letter; as you enter it, you become one with Him.

— A HASIDIC TEACHING

of the pew where his long legs could have some extra stretch room. Frankly, I was a little uncomfortable and annoyed. I thought it was irresponsible of Griff to stick me next to his senile grandfather with whom I had spent exactly twenty minutes. I felt that Griff and I should switch places. But I also knew better than to speak up.

And then, as so often happens when I am uncomfortable and annoyed, this seating arrangement turned out to be the best thing ever. I would later speak of the privilege of sitting next to Granddaddy Gatewood. I would say that God Himself had a hand in arranging the seating. Because sitting next to him I could see (and hear) that Dr. Gatewood, who might not even remember how to count to ten, remembered how to pray. The Lord's Prayer and the Apostles' Creed were somewhere in the foundation of his memory, beneath even his grandchildren's names.

I doubt that Dr. Gatewood ever thought of what he was doing, when he said the Lord's Prayer, as "liturgy." But he was, in fact, praying a liturgy, for liturgy happens any time we repeat one prayer over and over, week in and week out. Sometimes that prayer was written by someone else (in Dr. Gatewood's case, the liturgy was composed by Jesus). Even the

**"PEOPLE THINK THAT THEY PRAY TO GOD**.
But this is not the case. For prayer itself *is* of the
very essence of God."
— RABBI PINHAS OF KORZEC

little child laying herself down to sleep, praying the Lord her soul to keep, is praying a liturgy. Even my friend Meg, who left the too-liturgical Episcopal Church for a praise-song-singing, spontaneous-prayer-praying charismatic church, will, I suspect, discover that she is doing liturgy: After enough time, the rhythms of the praise songs and the (seemingly) spontaneous prayers will become familiar and even routine, a liturgy of its own.

One could, I suppose, ask some questions about Dr. Gatewood's praying. Did he understand the propositions he was asserting in the Creed? Maybe not, but then on many days I don't understand them either. I don't know whether he could have cogently analyzed the Lord's Prayer or explained the Trinity to whom it was directed. What I know is this: These words of prayer are among the most basic words Dr. Gatewood knows. When he has forgotten everything else, those words are the words he will have. Those words have formed his heart, and— regardless of what he feels or remembers on any particular morning—they continue to form his heart still.

# Discussion Questions

**1.** I mention, at the start of this chapter, that Jewish prayer is liturgical prayer, and that I learned how to pray in this way during my time at the synagogue. The *Shema* is the prayer that Jews are called to recite in the morning and evening: "Hear O Israel, the Lord your God, the Lord is One."

The rabbis of the Talmud understood that repeating liturgical prayers can be dull at times, and that sometimes people "tune out" the meaning of a prayer when one repeats the same words over and over:

"If one reads the Shema and repeats it, it is disgraceful. . . .

"Rav Pappa said to Rava: Perhaps the reason he is repeating the Shema is because at first he did not concentrate, and now he is concentrating. Why then, is he silenced?. . . [Rava] replied to [Rav Pappa]: Does one act as an acquaintance toward Heaven? If he does not concentrate, I shall strike him with a blacksmith's hammer until he does concentrate." What does this passage say about how the rabbis understood prayer?

In what ways in your own prayer life have you acted "as an acquaintance toward Heaven"?

**2.** There is a much-beloved story about a boy learning (and ultimately teaching others) how to pray. The only thing this poor, ignorant shepherd boy had ever learned was the Hebrew alphabet, the *aleph-bet*. Every day he would sing the *aleph-bet* to his sheep.

On Shabbat the boy and his father would go to the synagogue and sit in the back, with other poor and unschooled men. The boy could neither read the prayers nor sing the songs, but as he listened he felt happy to be part of the Jewish people.

One Shabbat, as the boy sat with his father in the synagogue, hearing the cantor chant the beautiful Hebrew prayers and remembering the alphabet he had learned from his mother, the boy was gripped with the desire to speak directly to God, like the men all around him in their prayer shawls. Filled with love for God, the boy began to recite the *aleph-bet*, first softly, then louder and louder.

> His father stopped him. "Be quiet!" he commanded in a loud whisper. "You don't know how to read the prayers. Stop talking nonsense. Show respect! You're in the synagogue."
>
> The boy sat quietly, but after a while he began again.
>
> Again the father stopped him. This time he put a hand on the boy's mouth and said, "The rabbi will hear you and throw us out for what you are doing. Sit without making a sound or I'll take you home."
>
> So the boy sat quietly. But how long could he sit there when all around him he saw and felt the holiness of the day?

All of a sudden, the boy started to recite the alphabet again, even louder than before. Then, faster than his father could catch him, he jumped up from his seat and ran to the *bimah*.

"*Rebono shel Olam*, Ruler of the Universe, I know I am only a child. I want so much to sing the beautiful prayers to you, but I don't know them. All I know is the *aleph-bet*. Please, dear God, take these letters of the alphabet and rearrange them to form the words that mean what I want to say to you and what is in my heart."

When the father, the rabbi, and the congregation heard the boy's words, tears formed in their eyes. Then they all joined him in reciting, "*aleph, bet, daled, gimmel, hey, vav. . . .*"

How does this little boy show us a picture of a heart that is open to God? What can we learn from him?

**3.** I share in this chapter that liturgical prayer has helped me to stay focused on God when it would be easier to fall back into myself and my own emotional state: "Liturgy is not, in the end, open to our emotional whims. It repoints the person praying, taking him somewhere else" (page 74). So even when I don't feel a thirst or longing for God, liturgical prayer points me back to God.

Jesus introduced the following prayer, commonly recited as "The Lord's Prayer," to his disciples when they asked him how to pray:

"He was praying in a certain place, and after he had finished, one of his disciples said to him, 'Lord, teach us to pray, as John taught his disciples.' He said to them, 'When you pray, say: Father, hallowed be your name. Your kingdom come. Give us each day our daily bread. And forgive us our sins, for we ourselves forgive everyone indebted to us. And do not bring us to the time of trial." [Lk. 11:1–4]

What does the liturgy of The Lord's Prayer suggest about God's character? How does the prayer focus our attention not on ourselves but on who God is? What does the prayer imply about the ultimate purpose of prayer?

**4.** The Apostle Paul instructs the church in Philippi about prayer: "Rejoice in the Lord always; again I will say, Rejoice. Let your gentleness be known to everyone. The Lord is near. Do not worry about anything, but in everything by prayer and supplication with thanksgiving let your requests be made known to God. And the peace of God, which surpasses all understanding, will guard your hearts and your minds in Christ Jesus." [Phil. 4:4–7]

What does this passage suggest about the shape your prayers might take?

**5.** I am encouraged that even when I do not know how to pray, "the Spirit helps us in our weakness; for we do not know how to pray as we ought, but that very Spirit intercedes with sighs too deep for words." [Rom. 8:26]

Have you felt weak in prayer? Have you ever experienced the Holy Spirit helping you to pray? How might you more robustly incorporate prayer into your life this week?

# SIX

# Guf

### Body

I am downtown, outside a little boutique called Pearl, a boutique I hardly ever enter because their clothes, like the biblical pearl, come at great price; but this particular day I am strolling around with Ginger and we notice the Pearl mannequin is sporting a most cute skirt. It is just past the knee, pale cotton affixed with grosgrain ribbon, sporty, summery, and oh-so-chic. "Oh, try it on," says Ginger. The skirt costs $182. "If I knew how to sew," I say to Ginger, "I could make that skirt for twenty bucks." "But you don't know how to sew," says Ginger, "so try it on."

I do. "This small does not fit," I sing to the saleslady. "Do you have a medium?"

The saleslady (I am sure she is sighing and rolling her eyes and annoyed) goes to the mannequin, which is wearing a medium.

"The medium," I say, "is a little snug." Actually, I cannot get it to zip.

This is the sort of store that does not carry a large.

"Ah, well," I say cheerfully, "think of the $182 dollars I just saved, thanks to my hips, which were designed to have babies." Then, when we are out of the store, I start to cry.

"Why are you crying?" says Ginger, who knows why I am crying.

"I'll never be thin again," I wail. "I used to be thin." I tell Ginger about the purple pedal-pushers I had just taken to Goodwill because they, too, were a tad tight. Ginger reminds me that I bought the pedal-pushers in tenth grade.

This shopping expedition was good proof that, though I believe God has something to say about human bodies, I generally tune God out and listen to *Cosmopolitan* instead. I'm pretty sure that God, if He called me to chat about my body, would say things like, "I like your body. I created your body, and if you have read the first chapter of Genesis lately, you might recall that I called Creation good." Still, when I'm staring in the dress-shop mirror, I generally wish my body—or at least a few pounds of it—would vanish.

This desire to diet is not just bad feminism. It is also bad faith, for the biblical story of the body is very different from the bodily stories *Cosmo* and *Maxim* tell. The magazines (and movies, TV shows, and advertising campaigns) speak of bodies that are both too important and not important at all. Scripture speaks of bodies that God created in His image, bodies that are both doing redemptive work and being redeemed.

Christians, it must be admitted, have not told that story very consistently. The history of Christianity and the body is one of anxiety and unease; Christianity has the words to offer a spirituality of the body, but the church hasn't always spoken those words.

Judaism, on the other hand, has much more clearly insisted that being a body is intimately bound up with being a follower of God. This understanding is expressed in one of the most basic Jewish rituals, the *bris*, the ritual circumcision of baby boys.

God commanded circumcision in Genesis 17 as a sign of the covenant between Abraham and the Lord, and in circumcision, Jews mark their bodies for God. Jews carry the marks of their covenant with Him in their very flesh. The *bris* suggests that we do religion with our souls and hearts and minds, but we also do religion with our bodies.

Judaism offers opportunities for people to inhabit and sanctify bodies and bodily practices. Jews link everyday bodily practices, like eating and drinking, to the service of God. Judaism even sees the undeniably bodily acts of urinating and defecating as an opportunity for spiritual growth. Jewish law—which generally encourages one to think about lofty, holy things at all times—forbids contemplating the sacred while in the bathroom. The *Shulchan Aruch*, the sixteenth-century codification of Jewish law, reminds readers that "while in the bathroom, it is forbidden to think of sacred matters. It is, therefore, best to concentrate on your business affairs and accounts, so that you might not be led to think of holy thoughts, or, God forbid, indulge in sinful thoughts. On the Sabbath, when it is forbidden to think of business, you should think of interesting things you have seen or heard about, or something similar." Still, the rabbis are eager to transform the bathroom experience into one that can edify and point toward the Creator. Says Rabbi Yehudah ha-Hasid, "When you are in the bathroom or bathhouse, remember how much uncleanness and filth exits from your body, and be humbled."

Judaism connects physical acts to spiritual practice without somehow suggesting that the spirit is superior to the body. Consider sex. Rabbinic sources suggest that the intention of sexual intercourse is unity with one's spouse and with God; but Judaism's recognition of the spirituality of sex does not come at the expense of sexual physicality. One rabbi made the point

---

**"BLESSED ARE YOU**, Hashem, our G-d, King of the
universe, Who formed man with wisdom and created within
him many openings and many hollows (cavities). It is obvious
and known before Your Throne of Glory that if but one of them
were to be ruptured or if one of them were to be blocked it
would be impossible to survive and to stand before You (even
for a short period of time). Blessed are You, Hashem, Who
heals all flesh and acts wondrously."

—A TRADITIONAL JEWISH PRAYER
SAID UPON GOING TO THE BATHROOM

(Note: Traditional Judaism sometimes uses the word *Hashem*,
which literally means "the Name," in place of any name for
God, out of reverence.)

---

plainly: Before sex, he taught, you should give thanks to God for
the pleasure that He created.

The same holds for eating. As Rabbi Abraham of Slonim
taught, "Contrary to what one might think, it is possible sometimes to come closer to God when you are involved in material
things like eating and drinking, than when you are involved
with 'religious' activities like Torah and prayer. Because when
the heart opens up due to . . . pleasure . . . then is the fit time to
come close to holiness."

Jews connect eating to God, not just through the dietary
codes of *kashrut* but also in the preparation of tables and
meals. The table laden with food is meant to recall the altar
of the Temple. (This has practical consequences that will be
pleasing to moms everywhere: According to a Hasidic teaching,
even clearing the table after a meal is a holy act, for it recalls

the priests' removing sacred spoons from the Holy of Holies.) Every morsel of food is blessed before being eaten, and Jews recite a lengthy grace after meals. A consistent theme in the traditional literature on eating is that the pleasure of good food can point back toward the Creator. There is a Hasidic tale of a rabbi who visited a very poor woman. She served him dinner, and the food was scrumptious. The rabbi, having enjoyed the meal tremendously, looked at the woman and declared, "This food tastes like heaven!" Smiling, the woman said, "That's

---

**ONCE, WHEN HILLEL** was taking leave of his disciples, they said to him: "Master where are you going?' He replied, "To do a pious deed." They asked, "What may that be?" He replied, "To take a bath." They said, "Is that a pious deed?" He replied, "Yes. If, in the theaters and circuses, the images of the king must be kept clean by the person to whom they have been entrusted, how much more is it a duty of a person to care for the body, since we have been created in the divine image and likeness." In a parallel situation, Hillel answered the disciples' question: "I am going to do a kindness to the guest in the house." When the disciples asked whether he had a guest every day, Hillel answered, "Is not my poor soul a guest in the body? Today it is here, tomorrow it is gone."

Have you ever thought about taking a bath as doing "a pious deed?" Why or why not? How do you usually think about your body—if you think about it at all? What words would you use to describe your body?

**THE TALMUD SAYS** "You should bathe your face, hands, and feet every day in honor of your Creator."

because while cooking I prayed that God would put the taste of the Garden of Eden in the meal." Physical pleasure provided a foretaste of eternity.

❧

The point is not that we'll know God simply because we experience fine dining. Jews know God because He has revealed Himself in the covenants, not in meals. Jews can appreciate meals, sex, and the body because they already know the God who made Creation. Because one knows the Creator, one can taste Him in the breaking of bread.

It is no accident that Jewish prayers relating to the body acknowledge, above all, God as Creator. The prayer to be uttered before sex thanks God for creating pleasure; similarly, the *asher yatzar*, the blessing Jews recite after going to the bathroom, thanks God for "creating in me many orifices and many cavities. It is obvious and known before Your throne of glory that if one of them were to be ruptured or one of them blocked, it would be impossible for a man to survive and stand before You." Jews can be present to their bodies in part because they have a story, and a doctrine, of Creation.

One must acknowledge an underbelly (to use a bodily metaphor) to this sanguine picture of Jews and bodies. Jews engage their bodies not simply because Jewish theology, the

Jewish teaching of Creation, suggests they ought, but also because the non-Jewish world has engaged Jewish bodies pathologically and prejudicially. Ideas about Jewish bodies have figured prominently in anti-Jewish and anti-Semitic tropes for centuries—beginning with the Christian idea, put forth most notably by Augustine, that Jews were inherently and basely corporal and bodily; their very carnality prevents them from apprehending the spiritual reality that is Jesus Christ. A more modern anti-Jewish topos insists on a particular Jewish physiognomy—the hooked nose, the full lips. In America, Jewish women's bodies have become the stuff of anti-Jewish fantasies; in a 1930 New York newspaper, to cite just one example, an anonymous columnist at once insisted that Jewish women spent more money on clothes and accessories than their Gentile counterparts, and excused Jewish women for the extravagance because "the Jewish girl must offset her . . . vulgar [figure] by making it her rule to wear the simplest clothes possible. [And] alas . . . the simplest clothes are the most expensive." If Christians have not developed the same vigorous enjoyment of the body that Judaism cultivates, that is surely in part because Christians have not been pushed, by caricature and perversion, to define, defend, and revel in their bodies.

Still, it is curious that Christians, in contrast to Jews, have such ambivalence about the body. The difference between Jewish and Christian understandings of the body is not as simple as the popular stereotype that Christians think the body is bad and Jews think the body is good. Rather, as scholar Daniel Boyarin puts it, "for rabbinic Jews, the human being was defined as a body—animated, to be sure, by a soul," whereas for early Christians "the essence of a human being is a soul housed in a body." Later Christians perpetuated an uneasiness about bodily matters, and by the modern era, Western Christians had become very much an Enlightenment people who liked to live Christianity in their minds rather than in their bodies. True enough, the church fathers labeled Gnosticism, with its insistence that spirit was separate from and superior to matter, a heresy; but, like most great heresies, Gnosticism has mutated and morphed and continued to dog Christianity. Even the most faithful Christians can sometimes catch themselves in a Gnostic mindset of wanting to deny, rather than rightly order, bodily desires for sex, food, even sleep.

This Christian discomfort with the body perplexes me. Christians, after all, share the story of Creation that seems to

---

**ORIGEN, THE THIRD-CENTURY THEOLOGIAN**, reminds us that: "In regard to our bodily nature we must understand that there is not one body which we now use in lowliness and corruption and weakness and a different one which we are to use hereafter in incorruption and power and glory. Rather this same body, having cast off the weaknesses of its present existence, will be transformed into a thing of glory and made spiritual, with the result that what was a vessel of dishonor shall itself be purified and become a vessel of honor and a habitation of blessedness."

What do you make of the idea that we will have bodies (or be bodies) for all eternity? What does that say about how God views the human body? Why do you think bodies are so important to God?

---

have provided Jews a rich resource for a robust realization of the body. And we have another story, too: the bodily Incarnation and bodily Resurrection of God. The New Testament makes clear that God cares about bodies very much indeed. He created us with bodies, He incarnated and took on a body, and He was resurrected in a body. We will be these bodies, albeit transformed, in the final Resurrection. Bodies are not mere trappings. They are the very stuff of us.

Attending Christianly to our bodies is a matter of some urgency, because there is no neutral way to be a body. If we do not take our bodily cues from the Christian story, we will take them from somewhere else—from the magazines screaming about taking off five pounds, from the all-you-can-eat buffets asking us to stuff our bodies, from the fashion designers asking us to parade them.

Yet to think of Christian practices of the body seems almost to ponder a contradiction in terms. In church, I sometimes kneel and raise my hands and bow my head. I decorate my body with cruciform jewelry. That's about it. I have not, apparently, managed a Christian attitude toward skirt size.

What I want is to pay more attention—and more explicitly theological attention—to my body and the things it does every day and the connections between the work of my body and the daily service of God. On the occasion when I linger over a meal for more than eight minutes (and it's no coincidence that those lingering evenings are also the evenings that I don't eat alone), supper, like the Communion table, can be an opportunity to meet God in the breaking of bread. Similarly, Disciples of Christ minister Stephanie Paulsell has suggested that we take our evening bath as an opportunity to ponder and pray into the baptismal covenant. I think this is a grand idea, although

**"THE MOVEMENT OF THE BODY** can generate the flow of consciousness and direct you. In fact, the Baal Shem Tov says that if you are particularly stuck in your prayer, you can accomplish that just by looking around at different things. Taking your eyes off whatever you're looking at now and looking somewhere else creates a new awareness in yourself."
—RABBI ETHAN FRANZEL

I haven't managed to implement it—to be honest, most days when I settle into my lavender bath foam, the last thing I'm thinking about is the morning I stood in the Clare College Chapel, renounced Satan, and accepted Christ.

Another realm to which the gospel might speak is exercise. Some Christians may cringe at the old Pauline insistence that "our bodies are the temple of the Holy Spirit"—the phrase has been so oft repeated as to seem trite, if not entirely denuded. But I must confess there are only two reasons I get up for my 7:30 exercise class: the knowledge that my friend Molly is there and will kill me if I don't show up, and the equally sure knowledge that Scripture enjoins me to care for my body. Does this mean that I think about Jesus with every jumping jack? Not at all. What it means is that my exercising is not merely a capitulation to a fitness-crazy culture, but rather is an attempt at obedience. God created this body of mine; the least I can do is try halfheartedly to take care of it. (Granted, I do this only once a week. God, it seems, is not finished transforming sedentary me into a new creature.)

**"WHEN I PRAY**, my body takes on a life of its own. Sometimes I sway horizontally, other times vertically. At times my hands are to my sides, at times they are in a beseeching position. There are times when they reach up, as if aspirating to reach where my words cannot go. I observe my hands, seeking to understand what it is that they are trying to tell me."

—REB MIMI FEIGELSON

Have you ever considered what might happen in your prayers if you allow your body to be central to your prayer? How might your bodily posture—or movement—during prayer help you attend to your prayers more actively? How might your body help you attend to God more consciously?

Then there is the matter of suffering. It is all well and good to urge Christians to be present to their bodies when they are eating a good meal or having great sex. But what does it mean to preach presence to one who is in bodily pain?

Lately, I've been thinking about bodies in pain, principally because I've been watching my mother's body deteriorate. She has uterine cancer—an especially invasive and aggressive kind of uterine cancer. The good news is the chemo seems to be working. The bad news is that when chemo works, the oncologists keep giving it to you, injecting you with just the right amount of poison (they hope) to kill the tumor but not kill you. First, naturally, her hair fell out. Then she simultaneously lost weight and got bloated (a sad thing to watch happen to the body of a woman who won legs contests in college). Then came peripheral neuropathy; in layman's terms, she has lost the feeling in her feet. She has begun to walk with a cane and has traded in her stick shift for an automatic.

I want her to read this chemo and cancer through gospel lenses—even as I am not entirely sure what that reading would look like. This is not to say that suffering is a Christian good, that suffering makes us holy and puts us closer to God (though, sometimes, making us holy may be one thing that suffering accomplishes). I remind her that the Incarnation culminates with Christ suffering on the Cross. When God became man He did not simply take on a body that was in the bloom of health. He took on a body destined for suffering, and His body now, as my mother's body one day will be, is resurrected and in heaven. The irony, I suppose, is that sometimes it may be our very bodily suffering that forces us to inhabit the bodies our culture has helped us alternately vilify and ignore. Catholic poet and memoirist Nancy Mairs has made the point when writing about multiple sclerosis: "Slowly, slowly," she writes, "MS will teach me to live as a body."

---

**ROWAN WILLIAMS**, an Anglican theologian and former Archbishop of Canterbury, has written, "Being a body is a spiritual discipline; just as being 'spiritual' is finding a way of living fully and gratefully as a body." How is "being a body" a spiritual discipline? What in your life is helping you find a way of "living fully and gratefully as a body"? What is interfering with your living that way?

---

The latest side effect of my mother's chemo is cosmetic: Her eyebrows have fallen out. (One lone brow hair remains over her right eye, and she takes this as a metaphor for tenacity.) Mom has penciled in orange crescents where her eyebrows should be, and when she asks if these new brows are too terribly obviously fake, I tell her it is nice that the bangs of her wig are so long.

I used to nag my mother about make-up. She is one of those Southern Ladies of a Certain Age who spend a good chunk of the morning preparing her face to meet the world. I've always found this ridiculous, and so once I confiscated all her lipstick. I tried to get her to read *The Beauty Myth*. To no avail.

Part of me still wishes she would take to the streets bald—some sort of political statement about women's health and women's bodies. But I am beginning to understand about the dignity and the art of the wigs and the makeup. This small, everyday attentiveness of eyebrow pencils is perhaps a picture of the very sort of bodily care our embodied God would have us cultivate whether in illness or wellness, whether our bodies are in the throes of ecstasy or the throes of pain.

# Discussion Questions

**1.** Consider the following from contemporary Jewish teacher Yitzhak Buxbaum:

> "I am going to take a bath to keep my body clean, for the honor of my Creator; for my body is His wondrous creation, the house of the soul, which is made in His image."

Then, put Buxbaum's words alongside this, which the Apostle Paul wrote to the church in Corinth:

> "Or do you not know that your body is a temple of the Holy Spirit within you, which you have from God, and that you are not your own? For you were bought with a price; therefore glorify God in your body."

If our bodies are made in the image of God and are temples of the Holy Spirit, how might it mean to truly inhabit our bodies?

**2.** Tertullian, an early Christian theologian and author, notes that, "In the Platonic view, the body is a prison; in that of Paul it is the temple of God because it is in Christ." Do you sometimes think of or experience your body as a prison? How does this affect your experience of God?

**3.** Consider this psalm:

> For it was you who formed my inward parts; you knit
> me together in my mother's womb. I praise you, for I
> am fearfully and wonderfully made. Wonderful are your
> works; that I know very well. My frame was not hidden
> from you, when I was being made in secret, intricately
> woven in the depths of the earth. Your eyes beheld my
> unformed substance. In your book were written all the
> days that were formed for me, when none of them as yet
> existed. [Ps. 139:13–16]

What does this Scripture passage say about God's
thoughts about the human body? What does it tell you about
your own body?

**4.** John's Gospel declares, "And the Word became flesh and
lived among us, and we have seen his glory, the glory as of
a father's only son, full of grace and truth" [Jn. 1:14]. What
does Jesus' experiencing life, death, and resurrection *in* and
as a *body* suggest about the importance of human bodies to
God?

**5.** Historian Peter Brown notes that "In Paul's letters, we are
presented with the human body as in a photograph taken
against the sun: it is a jet-black shape whose edges are

suffused with light. Perishable, weak, 'sown in dishonor,' 'always carrying the death of Jesus' in its vulnerability to physical risk and to bitter frustration, Paul's body was very much an 'earthen vessel.' Yet it already glowed with a measure of the same spirit that had raised the inert body of Jesus from the grave: 'so that the life of Jesus may be manifested in our mortal flesh.' The approach of that bright light threw dramatic shadows."

In what ways have you experienced, in your own body, the "perishable" and "weak" nature of the flesh? Do you ever wrestle with the limitations of your own body? What is most frustrating to you? Have you ever thought, in the moments of limitation, that your body is still "glow[ing] with a measure of the same spirit that" raised Jesus from the dead? How can we live well within the tension of these two realities?

**6.** One of the most intensely embodied stories in the New Testament is the story of the hemorrhaging woman. The Gospel of Mark tells the story this way:

> Now there was a woman who had been suffering from hemorrhages for twelve years. She had endured much under many physicians, and had spent all that she had; and she was no better, but rather grew worse. She had heard about Jesus, and came up behind him in the crowd and touched his cloak, for she said, "If I but touch his clothes, I will be made well." Immediately

her hemorrhage stopped; and she felt in her body that she was healed of her disease. Immediately aware that power had gone forth from him, Jesus turned about in the crowd and said, "Who touched my clothes?" And his disciples said to him, "You see the crowd pressing in on you; how can you say, 'Who touched me?'" He looked all around to see who had done it. But the woman, knowing what had happened to her, came in fear and trembling, fell down before him, and told him the whole truth. He said to her, "Daughter, your faith has made you well; go in peace, and be healed of your disease." [Mk. 5:25–34]

Although the NRSV says that the woman "felt" in her body she was healed, the Greek actually means she "knew" in her body. Jennifer Glancy, a historian of the early church, explains this: "The translator's shift from knowing to feeling conforms to commonplace usage. Bodies feel. Minds know. Mark, however, implies that bodies know, that we are capable of corporal knowledge. What do we know in the body? Mark's vignette of the bleeding woman suggests one simple answer. We know when we are sick and when we are well. We also know when the air is sticky and the very moment when a breeze cools the late afternoon. But . . . corporal knowledge is not limited to matters of health or sense perception. What else do we know in the body?" How would you answer Glancy's question? How do you think Jesus would answer?

✐

**7.** Christians believe that in the Incarnation, God, in a body, came to live among us. We don't always realize that there are descriptions of God's having a body long before the New Testament tells us about Jesus. As Hebrew Bible scholar Esther Hamori explains, twice in Genesis "God appears in concrete, tangible human form. God's appearance in these texts does not take place in a dream or a vision, and the language is not metaphorical. Rather, the narrators of these stories portray God as appearing in a physical human body." The two stories in question are these:

> The LORD appeared to Abraham by the oaks of Mamre, as he sat at the entrance of his tent in the heat of the day. He looked up and saw three men standing near him. When he saw them, he ran from the tent entrance to meet them, and bowed down to the ground. He said, "My lord, if I find favor with you, do not pass by your servant. Let a little water be brought, and wash your feet, and rest yourselves under the tree. Let me bring a little bread, that you may refresh yourselves, and after that you may pass on—since you have come to your servant." So they said, "Do as you have said." And Abraham hastened into the tent to Sarah, and said, "Make ready quickly three measures of choice flour, knead it, and make cakes." Abraham ran to the herd, and took a calf, tender and good, and gave it to the servant, who hastened to prepare it. Then he took curds and milk and the calf that he had prepared, and set it before them; and he stood by them under the tree while they ate. They said

to him, "Where is your wife Sarah?" And he said, "There, in the tent." Then one said, "I will surely return to you in due season, and your wife Sarah shall have a son." And Sarah was listening at the tent entrance behind him. Now Abraham and Sarah were old, advanced in age; it had ceased to be with Sarah after the manner of women. So Sarah laughed to herself, saying, "After I have grown old, and my husband is old, shall I have pleasure?" The LORD said to Abraham, "Why did Sarah laugh, and say, 'Shall I indeed bear a child, now that I am old?' Is anything too wonderful for the LORD? At the set time I will return to you, in due season, and Sarah shall have a son." But Sarah denied, saying, "I did not laugh"; for she was afraid. He said, "Oh yes, you did laugh." [Gen. 18:1–15]

-and-

The same night he got up and took his two wives, his two maids, and his eleven children, and crossed the ford of the Jabbok. He took them and sent them across the stream, and likewise everything that he had. Jacob was left alone; and a man wrestled with him until daybreak. When the man saw that he did not prevail against Jacob, he struck him on the hip socket; and Jacob's hip was put out of joint as he wrestled with him. Then he said, "Let me go, for the day is breaking." But Jacob said, "I will not let you go, unless you bless me." So he said to him, "What is your name?" And he said, "Jacob." Then the man said, "You shall no longer be called Jacob, but

Israel, for you have striven with God and with humans, and have prevailed." Then Jacob asked him, "Please tell me your name." But he said, "Why is it that you ask my name?" And there he blessed him. So Jacob called the place Peniel, saying, "For I have seen God face to face, and yet my life is preserved." The sun rose upon him as he passed Penuel, limping because of his hip. Therefore to this day the Israelites do not eat the thigh muscle that is on the hip socket, because he struck Jacob on the hip socket at the thigh muscle. [Gen. 32:22–32]

Why might the biblical writers have described God as having bodily form? What kind of friendship do you think might be possible between you and a God who is embodied? Is something possible in that friendship that would not be possible in a friendship with a not-embodied God?

# SEVEN

#  Tzum

### Fasting

**M**y priest has tried, on a few occasions, to talk to me about fasting. Was regular fasting part of my spiritual discipline? Did I fast on Good Friday? Did I fast on Ash Wednesday?

"I'm not really into fasting," I would say. "I don't know why fasting is so hard for me," I would sometimes add with an air of world-weariness. "When I practiced Judaism, of course, I fasted all the time."

Once, my priest tried to give me an out: "So do you think the reason you don't fast now, as a Christian, is because there is still an emotional tie, or a symbolic connection, or maybe just some unfinished business to do with Judaism?"

"Nope," I said, "I just don't really like to do it. To fast, that is."

Eventually, these conversations had to end, and the way they ended, finally, was my agreeing to try to fast on Fridays during Lent.

Fasting, in Judaism, is a given. On holidays such as the Day of Atonement or the Ninth of Av (which commemorates the destruction of the Temple), all observant adult Jews fast.

Indeed, the Jewish calendar designates no fewer than seven days that should be set aside for fasting. These fast days fall into one of two categories, the major fast and the minor fast. On a major fast, like the Day of Atonement, you fast a full twenty-five hours, from sunset to sunset, and you abstain not only from food and drink but also from anointing yourself and from sex. Also, you do not wear leather shoes, because leather is too comfortable for a fast day. This is why you will see many Jews in synagogue on the Day of Atonement, the holiest day of the year, dressed to the nines and wearing white tennies. The minor fast is shorter, just sunup to sundown, and only prohibits food and drink. And there are exceptions, of course. If you are ill, or pregnant, or nursing, or too elderly, or too young, you do not have to fast. If the fast falls on a Sabbath, it is suspended (except for Yom Kippur, which is the Sabbath of Sabbaths, and takes precedence even over the commandment to be joyful on Shabbat).

To be honest, I was never all that good at fasting. I generally kept the fasts, but I rarely seemed to do them well. Fasting is meant to take you, temporarily, out of the realm of the physical and focus your attention heavenward; as one Jewish guide to fasting puts it, "at the heart of this practice is a desire to shift our attention away from our immediate needs and to focus on more spiritual concerns." But I usually found myself more, not less, obsessed with my belly. And, once or twice, I skipped or ignored or broke a fast. My freshman year of college, for example, I got distractingly hungry on the Fast of Esther. And so at about two o'clock I ate a salami sandwich. Actually, the story is worse than that: Not having any food in my dorm room, I found the key to the campus kosher deli where I worked (it was of course closed because of the fast day) and made my salami sandwich there.

**IN THE FOURTH AND FIFTH CENTURIES**, some devout Christian men and women lived in caves and huts in the deserts; they had fled the lures and glamour of the city in order to try to focus on God. They fasted, and some of their teachings about fasting were eventually written down:

Once two brothers went to visit an old man. It was not the old man's habit, however, to eat every day. When he saw the brothers, he welcomed them with joy, and said: "Fasting has its own reward, but if you eat for the sake of love, you satisfy two commandments, for you give up your own will and also fulfill the commandment to refresh others."

A brother said to an old man: "There are two brothers, of whom one remains praying in his cell, fasting six days at a time and doing a great deal of penance. The other one takes care of the sick. Which one's work is more pleasing to God?" The old man replied: "If that brother who fasts six days at a time were to hang himself up by the nose, he could not equal the one who takes care of the sick." Here we learn that love is above fasting, that we must not presume to put our fasting above "the more excellent way," the "new commandment" to love one another.

A leader of a community asked Abba Poemen: "How can I acquire the fear of God?" Abba Poemen replied: "How can we acquire the fear of God when our belly is full of cheese and preserved foods?" Abba Poemen thus teaches us that the ultimate goal of fasting is to help lead us, or to open us, to the fear of God.

If the only thing you knew about God and spirituality
came from those three desert teachings, how would you
describe God and life with God?

∽

There is a long history of Christian fasts, beginning with
those fasts observed by Jesus Himself. Jesus' most stunning
fast came in the desert, where He fasted for forty days. At
the end of the forty days, the devil came and tempted Him
with power and glory and riches, and Jesus withstood the
Adversary, saying "Get thee behind me, Satan." The Gospel of
Luke suggests that though perhaps physically weakened from
His fast, Jesus was spiritually much stronger for it, and, indeed,
the fast helped give Him the moxie to renounce the devil. A
curious and paradoxical-seeming, even impossible-seeming,
lesson: fasting won't just make you headachy and irritable and
ravenous. It will make you, somehow, stronger. Jesus seemed
to assume that fasting was an essential part of the spiritual
life—He said to His disciples, "When you pray, when you
fast, and when you give alms," not *if* you fast, but *when*. And
the Gospel of Matthew makes this scary, flat claim: There are
demons that "go not out but by prayer and fasting."

Fasting was a central discipline to the early church and on
through the Middle Ages, but people fell away from fasting
after the Reformation. At least in Protestant churches, fasting
has been generally reduced to Lenten observance—some people abstain from food on the Fridays of Lent; others make a

mini-fast for the entire period, giving up chocolate or alcohol or restaurants. The strong hold of the Lenten fast returns to Jesus in the desert, for during Lent we both recall and recapitulate His forty days there. During Lent we also repent, and as the rabbis say, fasting is at its core about repentance.

Though since the Second Vatican Council American bishops have stripped the act of obligatory status, many Catholics have retained the practice of abstaining from meat on Fridays. These Friday fasts recall, weekly, the suffering of Christ on the Cross. Eastern Orthodox Christian communities, it seems, understand and inhabit fasting best. During Lent, for example, they completely abstain from all meat, dairy, and egg products. The Orthodox also fast on Sunday mornings, refraining even from drinking a cup of coffee until they have partaken of Holy Communion, feeding on the body and blood of Christ before they indulge in a croissant or a stack of pancakes.

In recent years some American Protestants have begun to recover this venerable Christian practice. As journalist Christine Gardner has written, "American evangelicals [are] rediscovering fasting, among the most ancient and rigorous of spiritual disciplines." Whole communities have taken up fasting for repentance, fasting for discernment, fasting for purification. Two examples will illustrate: In 1998, two million people tuned in, via the Internet, to a Campus Crusade for Christ conference on fasting and prayer, and the following year the National Association of Evangelicals promoted forty days of fasting and prayer for its 43,000 member churches.

Contemporary Christian enthusiasm for fasting has included a creative and capacious notion of what it means to fast. Increasingly, Christians think of fasts not simply as abstentions from food, but abstentions from all manner of indulgence.

**CATHOLIC HISTORIAN EAMON DUFFY** argues
that, in giving up fasting, Christians have lost something
important. "The whole rationale of symbolic gestures
requires that they disrupt and disturb the secular order.
Their power to witness—not only to others but to
ourselves—comes precisely from their awkwardness.
The abolition of such observances strikes at the heart
of tradition, the distinctive language of belief," writes
Duffy. "[I]n our march into the needs and opportunities of
the twenty-first century we should . . . try once more to
summon up some of the deeper resources of our own
tradition, and try to rediscover within it once more some
of the supports which helped our fathers and mothers
to live the gospel. We could do worse than rededicate
ourselves to the observance of fasting and abstinence."

Have you ever fasted? What did you notice about the
experience of fasting?

Catherine Marshall, the charismatic writer best known for her
novel *Christy*, once fasted from offering criticism. In *A Closer
Walk,* she describes her surprise at the number of times she
simply had to stay silent because she had nothing non-critical
to say, and then again her surprise at how little her usual
contributions were missed. (Though Marshall probably wasn't
thinking of it, there is a medieval Jewish precedent for her
criticism fast—the *tzom shtikah,* or the fast of silence, in which
Jewish mystics refrained from speaking, and, in their stillness
contemplated the mysteries of the divine.)

These non-gastronomic fasts can, no doubt, be edifying and instructive, but I suspect that a criticism fast, however difficult, would be easier for me than a food fast, and I suspect that I would be pretty tempted to use the cunning and spiritual-sounding criticism/TV/shopping/etc. fast as a justification for avoiding the basic discipline of abstaining from food.

So my priest has asked me to fast on Fridays during Lent, and that is what I have tried to do. Some Fridays are better than other Fridays. Some Fridays are okay, and other Fridays are irksome. One Friday I got a headache I couldn't shake. On another Friday I scooped out half a bowl of chocolate chip ice cream before I remembered. On still another Friday, I seemed to be praying better than I had prayed in a long, long time, but I am not sure that the fast had anything to do with the fortitude

---

**WHEN RAV SHEISHESS**, one of the Talmudic rabbis, fasted, he said this prayer: "Master of the Worlds, it is revealed before You that at the time the Holy Temple stood a person who sinned would offer a sacrifice, and he would offer from it only its fat and its blood; and, nevertheless, [that] alone would atone for him. And now, when the Temple is no longer standing, I have engaged in fasting, and my own fat and blood have been diminished. May it be Your will that my fat and my blood that are diminished be regarded as if I had offered them before You upon the Altar, and may You show me favor."

---

of my prayers: It might be coincidence. People who have fasted for years tell me there will come a time when I look forward to fasting—they tell me that there will come a time when I chafe under the church's insistence that one not fast during Christmas or Easter, seasons wholly given over to feasting. I am willing to believe that those times may come, but they are not here yet.

There are, of course, practical ways to make fasting less difficult. I have figured out that I always get hungry around two o'clock (the Hour of the Salami Sandwich), and if I'm willing to sweat it out till about 3:30, I'll be okay until dinner. And my beloved priest has told me that, just as Judaism makes allowances for circumstances that would make fasting too burdensome, so does Christianity. Not simply if you are sick or nursing or infirm, but also, says my priest, if you are unavoid- ably with people. That is to say, when your grandparents are passing through town and expect to take you to Bizou for lunch on Friday, you are to suspend your fast and go to Bizou, because going is the hospitable thing to do, and the communal practice of hospitality, judiciously understood, trumps your own private devotion.

Even in this early relearning of fasting, I can begin to see that Jesus expects us to fast not because He is arbitrary or capricious or cruel, but because fasting does good work on both our bodies and our souls. One Jewish fasting manual instructs its readers to slow down during fast days, to accept that our bodies will not move and our synapses will not click and our brains will not process quite as quickly. (In this way, "fast" sometimes seems like a misnomer.) It's a basic point, but one that bears repeating: Fasting is to be, as St. Thomas Aquinas once wrote, "a perfect quieting of all our impulses, fleshly and spiritual." Fasting is not meant to drag us down, but to still us. It is not meant to

**BASIL THE GREAT**, a fourth-century bishop of Caesarea, notes that fasting should not only affect our bodies, but also our hearts: "Take heed that you do not make fasting to consist only in abstinence from meats. True fasting is to refrain from vice. Shred to pieces all your unjust contracts. Pardon your neighbors. Forgive them their trespasses."

distract us from the really real, but rather to silence us so that we can hear things as they most truly are.

After that salami sandwich Fast of Esther episode, I rang up my rabbi. I asked him how important these minor fasts were. I asked him if I would ever get any better at them. I asked him what the point was. "Take Yom Kippur," I said. "Yom Kippur is the holiest day of the year. It is a day during which you should focus every iota of your attention on God. Wouldn't it be easier to do that if you had eaten a bowl of cereal at nine A.M., and so weren't thinking about your hunger pangs all day?"

Rabbi M. did not roll back thousands of years of rabbinic instruction and tell me to eat a bowl of Chex on the morning of Yom Kippur. Instead, he said the hunger was part of the point. "When you are fasting," he said, "and you feel hungry, you are to remember that you are really hungry for God."

And that has become my litany, my chant. When I sit at my desk on a Friday afternoon and wonder whether one little blue corn tortilla chip with a dab of black bean spread would really hurt, I say the words out loud: *I am hungriest for God, my truest hunger is for God.*

That litany tells me what fasting is. It is not merely a long, torturous means to a far-away end; a fast is not to be understood

**CHRISTIAN ETHICIST** and Methodist pastor Amy Laura Hall has questioned whether, in a society afflicted with gendered eating disorders, women should adopt the spiritual practice of fasting. Maybe they should adopt the spiritual practice of eating:

> I was lecturing years ago on Thomas Aquinas's understanding of virtue as the mean between two extremes, and on the various penitential practices for graced habituation. Some of the precious students looking back at me had told me during office hours that they were struggling with self-cutting and/or anorexia, and a few of them were also in abusive relationships with young men who were not only *not* worth these women's beautiful time, but who also had no interest in truly loving these women in their gorgeous vulnerability. I might have stuck my nose back into my notes, and plowed forward, but I just couldn't. I stopped the planned lecture and improvised. I suggested, totally off the cuff, that women who struggle with anorexia should eat chocolate covered strawberries every day of Lent. People laughed a bit, but I warmed to the idea. As a Lenten practice, in order to habituate toward the mean of temperance, some women, and perhaps some men too, might need to eat exactly what they fear, but should love, in order to open themselves to God's blessing in their student kitchenettes. I stopped there, but I probably should have continued. I should have talked to them about how ritually submitting to male authority was likely to keep them stuck with a mere mortal, rather than lead them to the Word made flesh. But, it was a beginning.

What do you think of Amy Laura Hall's analysis?

as a miserable experience that will eventually sanctify you. Nor is a fast like a back-room deal at the courthouse, the lawyer for the penitent trading three weeks of food in exchange for divine mercy. Rabbi M.'s words make clear that, like the liturgy, the fast accomplishes a repositioning. When I am sated, it is easy to feel independent. When I am hungry, it is possible to remember where my dependence lies.

# Discussion Questions

**1.** Sister Joyce Ann Zimmerman notes that fasting can draw us more closely to God: "Sacramental fasting does not posit a dualism between this world and the next—depriving ourselves of something of this world as something to be shunned in order to enter the next world. Instead, a sacramental approach to fasting links the reality of this world with the reality of the spiritual world. The obvious paradigm for this is the incarnation where the Second Person of the Trinity takes on human flesh, a perfect marriage between divinity and humanity. As the Son 'fasted' ('emptied,' to use the word of Phil 2:7) from his divinity and united himself with our humanity, he opened the way for things of this world to be truly sacramental, to be truly visible signs of invisible reality. The Son is the Sacrament *par excellence*. His incarnation opens the door for us to use such a simple practice as fasting to teach us to hunger for what is essential for us to have life itself: God who chooses to gift us with divine life."

How can the model of Jesus' "fasting" from divinity help us in our own discipline of fasting? How does the model of Jesus fasting show us our truest need, which is for God?

How, mysteriously, do we participate in Christ's very nature when we abstain from food for spiritual purposes?

**2.** In the Jewish tradition, fasting is a crucial part of one's friendship with God. In the Hebrew Bible, people fasted for a variety of reasons. King David, for example, fasted when he was grieving over the death of Saul and Jonathan: "Then David took hold of his clothes and tore them; and all the men who were with him did the same. They mourned and wept, and fasted until evening for Saul and for his son Jonathan, and for the army of the LORD and for the house of Israel, because they had fallen by the sword" (2 Sam. 1:11–12).

He also fasted for his enemies: "But as for me, when they were sick, I wore sackcloth; I afflicted myself with fasting. I prayed with head bowed on my bosom, as though I grieved for a friend or a brother; I went about as one who laments for a mother, bowed down and in mourning" (Ps. 35:13–14).

When the Hebrew Bible prophet Ezra was leading people from Babylon to Jerusalem, he proclaimed a fast: "Then I proclaimed a fast there, at the river Ahava, that we might deny ourselves before our God, to seek from him a safe journey for ourselves, our children, and all our possessions.

For I was ashamed to ask the king for a band of soldiers and cavalry to protect us against the enemy on our way, since we had told the king that the hand of our God is gracious to all who seek him, but his power and his wrath are against all who forsake him. So we fasted and petitioned our God for this, and he listened to our entreaty." (Ezra 8:21–23)

And when the Israelites had sinned against the Lord by taking foreign wives, it is recorded in the book of Nehemiah that they fasted: "Now on the twenty-fourth day of this month the people of Israel were assembled with fasting and in sackcloth, and with earth on their heads. Then those of Israelite descent separated themselves from all foreigners, and stood and confessed their sins and the iniquities of their ancestors. They stood up in their place and read from the book of the law of the Lord their God for a fourth part of the day, and for another fourth they made confession and worshiped the Lord their God." (Neh. 9:1–3)

In these Scriptures, we see numerous reasons that people fasted—to grieve, to pray for others, to ask God for protection, and to repent from sin. Now, look back over the Scripture passages above. Why, do you think, was fasting an appropriate response in each of these circumstances?

**3.** Christian Bible scholar Scot McKnight writes about David's decision to fast:

> For David, as for everyone in the Bible, prayer was *whole-body activity*, the way some Christians raise their hands

in worship or kneel on kneelers during confession time. My favorite writer about the Psalms, John Goldingay, tells us that David's sadness was not yet fully bloomed until the body—in this case, fasting—was involved: "The psalm assumes that merely to feel sadness is not enough; because we are physical creatures and not just minds and spirits, it would be odd not to express sorrow in (e.g.) abstention from food and then afflicting one's spirit and one's self."

What is your response to this idea that sadness is not fully "bloomed" in a person until their body participates in that emotion through fasting? How do you think this connection between spirit and body—through fasting—helped the Israelites repent from sin, in the book of Nehemiah? Or how did fasting engage the Israelites more wholeheartedly in asking God for protection, in the book of Ezra?

**4.** Here is Jesus' forty-day fast, as described in the Gospel of Matthew:

> Then Jesus was led up by the Spirit into the wilderness to be tempted by the devil. He fasted forty days and forty nights, and afterwards he was famished. The tempter came and said to him, "If you are the Son of God, command these stones to become loaves of bread." But he answered, "It is written, 'One does not live by bread alone, but by every word that comes from the mouth of God.'"

Then the devil took him to the holy city and placed him on the pinnacle of the temple, saying to him, "If you are the Son of God, throw yourself down; for it is written, 'He will command his angels concerning you,' and 'On their hands they will bear you up, so that you will not dash your foot against a stone.'" Jesus said to him, "Again it is written, 'Do not put the Lord your God to the test.'"

Again, the devil took him to a very high mountain and showed him all the kingdoms of the world and their splendor; and he said to him, "All these I will give you, if you will fall down and worship me." Jesus said to him, "Away with you, Satan! for it is written, 'Worship the Lord your God, and serve only him.'" Then the devil left him, and suddenly angels came and waited on him. (Matt. 4:1–11)

What does Jesus' fast show us about His relationship with God? What does it show us about His experience of His own body?

5. Middle-class America is shot through with an ambivalence about—and even disdain for—women's flesh. Many women are taught to believe, from a young age, that they should diet, and try to take up as little space as possible. In this context—as suggested by the passage from Amy Laura Hall on page 111—might be the very opposite of a spiritual practice that will draw the practitioner closer to God. For many women, fasting may present not an opportunity for spiritual

growth, but a method of cloaking unhealthy, disordered eating. Scholar Michelle Lelwica, attempting to minimize the likelihood of a toxic intersection between fasting and eating disorders, calls for fasting to engage "both our bodies and spirits in the process of self-transformation." Fasting as a spiritual disciple reconnects "people to their bodies, to their communities, and to their most sacred values." Lelwica contrasts this picture of fasting with disordered motivations to fast, including anxiety and control. Instead of using fasting to reject, shame, or dishonor one's body, Lelwica invites us to imagine fasting as a transformative practice. How might you rethink fasting in light of broader concerns of disordered eating? How do you think you might cultivate a holistic fasting that seeks to honor your body and the bodies of others? Or do you think that Lelwica's vision is virtually impossible in a culture beset by eating disordered and pernicious narratives about women's bodies? How might the passage by Amy Laura Hall complicate the church's teaching about and practice of fasting?

# EIGHT

# Hiddur p'nai zaken

## Aging

D o you have a section on aging?" I asked the woman at the information desk of the bookstore. I had already searched the health, family, and self-help sections. I was looking for a book for Lucy, a seventy-two-year-old woman I sometimes visit. She had read May Sarton's *At Seventy* and asked me to bring her something else in that vein.

"Nope," said the cheerless bookseller. "No aging section, but we do have quite a few books on aging over here." She led me to a bookshelf marked "beauty." There, jumbled up amongst *Beauty Secrets for Dummies* (foreword by the Duchess of York) and *The Beauty Bible,* were, after a fashion, a bunch of books about getting old: books with titles like *Battling Your Wrinkles* and *Looking Phenomenal after Fifty.* "These," I said, "seem to all be books about fighting the cosmetic effects of aging." I flipped one open to a discussion of age-spot removal: "Try lemon juice," the book instructed, as though written for a pre-teen nervous about freckles. I did not think age-spot removal was what Lucy wanted.

There is a *midrash* that speaks to this impulse to lemon-juice away your age spots. Once upon a time, the *midrash* says, adults of all ages looked the same—there were no crows' feet, no flabby upper arms, no sagging breasts or thinning hairlines.

But eighty-year-olds passing for thirty posed a problem: Whenever Abraham and his son Isaac went out together, no passersby could tell that Abraham was the elder—and since they couldn't tell he was old, they couldn't offer him the honor and reverence due to the elderly. So Abraham asked God to "crown him" with age spots and gray whiskers.

That *midrash* tells us something of how Judaism traditionally understands aging. The aged are not to be dismissed or ignored, but honored. Indeed, so central is that notion of honoring our elders that it finds its way to the middle of the Ten Commandments: "Honor thy father and thy mother." The same sentiment is reiterated and made more general in Leviticus 19:32 (NIV): "Rise in the presence of the aged, show respect for the elderly and revere your God."

Over the centuries, the rabbis have spelled out just what "respect" and "honor" require. The young are not to contradict anything their elders say. We are to stand whenever in the presence of someone who is elderly, even if that person is not especially wise or good or learned. Thirtysomethings are not permitted to take the most comfortable chair or sofa, but are to leave it empty in case an older person should enter the room.

A contemporary Jewish poet, Danny Siegel, has offered a creative reading of the biblical injunctions about the elderly. Poetic license firmly in hand, he translates the verse in Leviticus: "You shall rise before an elder and allow the beauty, glory, and majesty of their faces to emerge." We are obligated, says Siegel, "to provide whatever is best suited to the personal needs and desires of the elderly."

That may mean something simple, like bringing your older neighbor the latest John Grisham in large print or heading to Target and buying one of those digital alarm clocks with the honkingly huge red numbers for your dad. Or providing for the elderly's needs may be more demanding. It may mean caring for them at home while they die. It may mean, as it meant for my grandmother thirty years ago, converting your empty-nest spare bedrooms into an apartment for your elderly mom. It may mean, as it meant for my sister, driving that same grandmother, now an octogenarian, to Florida the year she finally decides she probably shouldn't drive herself.

It must be acknowledged that this giving care can be burdensome. It can be draining and hard. Perhaps the most essential insight of the Jewish approach to caring for one's elderly is that this care is, indeed, an obligation. What Judaism understands is that obligations are good things. They are the very bedrock of the Jew's relationship to God, and they govern some of the most fundamental human relationships: parent to child, husband to wife (and wife to husband, of course).

Somehow, though, when it comes to caring for the old, we disdain the notion of obligation. In one book I read recently, for example, the author  explains that when she grows old, she hopes her children will spend time with her only when they want to: "I don't ever want to be an obligatory visit on my loved one's calendars. . . . Whenever Robin and Edward visit Gramy Gert . . . they do so with no sense of duty. They look forward to spending time with her." I am thrilled that Robin and Edward enjoy their time with their grandmother so much, but the simple reality is that caring for our elderly, just like wiping our

**HERE ARE THE FIRST AND FIFTH** stanzas of John
Rippon's eighteenth-century hymn "How Firm a Foundation."
(As you read, remember that the word "hoary" can be "very
old" or "gray" or "gray-white.") What does the hymn suggest
about aging?

> How firm a foundation, ye saints of the Lord,
> Is laid for your faith in His excellent word!
> What more can He say than to you He hath said,–
> You who unto Jesus for refuge have fled?

> Even down to old age all my people shall prove
> My sovereign, eternal, unchangeable love
> And when hoary hairs shall their temples adorn
> Like lambs they shall still to my bosom be borne.

babies' bottoms and forgiving our spouses, is not always going
to be something we look forward to.

My mother is not yet elderly, but she is sick, and her cancer has required some caretaking on my part. To be honest, I
don't usually enjoy folding her laundry or flipping her mat-
tress or running to the pharmacy for her prescriptions, and I
don't always enjoy visiting with her. I do not look after Mom
because it is consistently easy and delightful. I do it because
I am obligated. I do it because of all the years she looked
after me. This is a sort of holy looking-after. It is not always
fun, but it is always sanctifying. And in this way, perhaps,
caretaking is something of a synecdoche of the spiritual life:
Most good and holy work (like praying and being attentive

**IN 1999,** the Episcopal Diocese in Maryland's Committee on Aging pulled together wise words and prayer about aging as a spiritual practice. Of the many riches they compiled, here are my three favorites:

> O God of unconditional and eternal love, you who give and sustain life in all its seasons, help us as we grow older to understand and affirm ourselves in our changing relationships with parents and others dear to us. Increase our sensitivity to their anxieties and frustrations. Give us thankful hearts for their love and nurture through the years. Grant us grace to forgive hurtful memories; and forgive us, Lord for our unloving words and deeds. Calm our fears of loss and change, and open our hearts to the promise of new life in Jesus' Name. AMEN.
>
> —BARBARA BROWN

> O God, our times are in your hands. Look with favor, we pray, on all your servants as our days increase. Grant that we may grow in wisdom and grace, and strengthen our trust in your goodness all the days of our lives; through Jesus Christ, our Lord. AMEN.
>
> —BOOK OF COMMON PRAYER, ADAPTED

> Put it firmly in your mind before you move that you will accept life and people as you find them—the stupid, the bright, the boring and garrulous (those who talk non-stop and interrupt your bright comment that you never get to make). Keep in mind that these strange folk are all loved

by God. And don't be upset by snappy or sour people
at breakfast: they probably have a pain somewhere and
seeing you apparently without one, drives them nuts. If
someone has something to say, or wants to confide a
problem, do listen. Smother your own impatience as best
you can with things as they are. Reach out and touch
when you might feel the urge to strike out. . . . One last
thought. Pray about this before you move. "What is my
mission in such a community? Is it real to me, and for
me?" If it's to love your neighbor as Christ loves—care
what happens to her/him—so that you can accept and
forgive, enjoy that funny one across the table—then you
needn't be bored or unhappy. You have a mission. It's
important at any age, but for an oldster, it's vital to have a
sense of mission. It's life-giving and life-long.

—EXCERPT FROM A LETTER OF ONE RECENTLY
MOVED TO A RETIREMENT HOME

How might your spiritual life be different if you prayed any
or all of these three prayers?

---

and even marching for justice or serving up chili at the soup
kitchen) is sometimes tedious, but these tasks are burning
away our old selves and ushering in the persons God has
created us to be.

Plus, of course, caring for another person can sometimes be
exceptionally straight forwardly rewarding. It can sometimes
be the best thing ever. Tonight I stopped by the health-food store
and decided to buy my mother an avocado. It is just a small
piece of green fruit, and it might not even appeal to her chemo

appetite, but it was good and simple and even joyful to bring it home to her all the same.

∽

We young folks are supposed to care for and respect our elders—that is the starting point for both Jewish and Christian teachings about the old. But both traditions also speak to those who are aging themselves. The elderly are asked to age well, and the communities that support them are asked to help them do just that. (Rabbi Zalman Schacter-Shalomi has dispensed with the gerund "aging." He speaks instead of "eldering." I'll admit a certain squeamishness with the term—it strikes me as a little twee, and every time I think of it, I have to adjust. But there is something vigorous about it too. To age is to be passive, to sit like a bottle of wine—you just sit there and time passes and age happens over you. To elder—or, in another of Reb Zalman's clever infinitives, "to sage"—is to try to shape the last years of one's life with intention.)

Aging is not just a process of physical decline. It can also be a time of the kind of stripping away that fosters spiritual depth, spiritual incline. The Hebrew word *sayvah,* gray—as in gray hair—is etymologically connected to the word for repentance, *teshuva:* The process of aging, then, is the process of setting wrong things right.

In the Middle Ages, in particular, Christians spoke of aging as, in the words of historian Shulamith Shahar, "an opportunity for spiritual elevation." John Bromyard, author of a fourteenth-century preaching guide, was not unique in holding the view that "in so far as old age reduces . . . youthful vigor, it increases the soul's devotion to God." Twenty-first-century

**SCHOLAR CONNIE L. SCARBOROUGH** writes about aging in Christian communities in the Middle Ages. In Europe, before the arrival of Christianity, women were understood to inhabit three different life stages (young, mature and old), and the old women were revered for their wisdom. But, according to Scarborough, when Christianity came to Europe, people began to lose their sense of women occupying these three distinct life stages and they began to lose their respect for old women. Increasingly, "women were relegated to essentially two acceptable roles—the virgin and the mother—these two conveniently conflated in the figure of the Virgin Mary, forever beautiful and pure whose body never suffered the ravages of old age and death." In this context, the old woman "was relegated to the margins of society and her wisdom became an object of fear. Her blighted youth became synonymous with ugliness and the signs of aging were believed to be physical manifestations of her sins and transgressions."

Do you think that women have different experiences of aging than men? What do you think of Scarborough's suggestion that Christianity is in some way responsible for killing off the wise, respected old woman, and replacing her with an ugly old woman best avoided?

Christians should not, perhaps, adopt the medieval view without criticism—the medieval thinker's understanding of the aging body was bound up with ambivalence about all bodies. Nor should the spiritual opportunities of aging distract the church from the sometimes difficult social and economic realities that face the elderly. Still, at the core of the medieval vision is the understanding that aging is not just about joints and wrinkles and families and hearing aids. It is also about prayer and attention and preparation and God.

The spirituality of aging inevitably involves preparing for one's death. A few years ago at Thanksgiving dinner, my father's first cousin—a man my father's age, about sixty— pushed back from the table, full from his Derby Pie and turkey stuffing, headed to the front door, and collapsed. Cousin Gene, it turned out, was in good health—perhaps he collapsed because he'd eaten too much, perhaps he'd simply been exhausted. But in the moments before the doctors declared Gene fit and fine, a very particular look passed over the faces of my father and uncle. They were both imagining that Gene had had a stroke, which seems to be the Angel of Death's favorite tool when it comes to the Winner family. As my sister Leanne described it, "You could see them thinking, *It's started. Our generation just began to die.*"

The very old often say they have made their peace with death, but few of us have that equanimity at thirty or forty or fifty. The very process of making peace is part of the opportunity that aging affords.

It is worth noting that through the nineteenth century, Americans' idea of a good death was one in which you lingered; you grew ill and knew death was imminent and thus you had time to settle accounts, with your debtors and your family and also your Maker. It is only in this last century that Americans have wished to be caught unawares in our sleep, looking for a death that is quick and painless and, also, a death for which we cannot prepare.

Christianity and Judaism both offer narratives that make sense of death, but they do not explain it away. No one who has encountered death can deny that it is disordered. Scripture understands that disordering as a result—a punishment—of the Fall. And the Christian narrative tells us that Jesus comes to rectify the Fall, to restore the order of Creation, to triumph over death. In Paul's magnificent summary, "Just as sin entered the world through one man, and death through sin, and in this way death came to all men . . . so also the result of one act of righteousness [the Incarnation, death and Resurrection of Christ] was justification that brings life for all men." This isn't a papering over. This doesn't mean that faithful Christians aren't scared of death—of course we are. In her book *Getting Over Getting Older,* Letty Cottin Pogrebin titles one chapter "Death and the Future—Not Necessarily in That Order." But for those of us who profess resurrection of the dead, we know that is indeed the necessary order.

In the 1970s, an anthropologist named Barbara Myerhoff spent several years studying an elderly Jewish community in Venice, California. Her book *Number Our Days* depicts men and women who were scraping by on small fixed incomes; many were in declining health; many died before Myerhoff's book was published. But the elderly people Myerhoff chronicled were also independent, resilient, imaginative, and often

**ROWAN WILLIAMS** writes this about the ways society treats the elderly: "It is of course a fact that advancing age is likely to decrease physical independence in various ways. But rather than taking this as the core issue, we should see questions of dependency as basically about how our public policy and resourcing seeks to preserve both dignity and capacity among those who may be increasingly physically challenged but remain citizens capable of contributing vital things to the social fabric. . . . We tolerate a very eccentric view of the good life or the ideal life as one that can be lived only for a few years between, say, eighteen and forty. The 'extremes' of human life, childhood and age, when we are not defined by our productive capacity, and so have time to absorb the reality around us in a different way—these are hard for our society to come to terms with. Too often we want to rush children into pseudo-adulthood; too often we want older citizens either to go on as part of the productive machine as long as possible or to accept a marginal and humiliating status, tolerated but not valued, while we look impatiently at our watches, waiting for them to be 'off our hands'. The recovery of a full and rich sense of dignity at every age and in every condition is an imperative if we are serious about the respect we universally owe each other, that respect grounded for Christians in the divine image which is to be discerned in old and young alike."

Williams is identifying productivity, dependence, and independence as registers about which we think about aging. How do you feel about possibly becoming more dependent in the future? What might one learn about God when one looks for the divine image in an old person?

happy. In Myerhoff's words, they "participat[ed] . . . in an active social life and enjoy[ed] a culture built out of a cherished common past."

Did the old Jews in Venice, California, do aging so well because of the textual imperatives of rabbinic Judaism? Not directly. What set them apart was that they lived within a community and a tradition that could help them remember who they were. Myerhoff didn't chronicle individual Jews living atomized lives on the West Coast; the elderly at Aliyah Senior Citizens' Center came together regularly for shared meals, classes in Jewish literature, the occasional prayer service. They spoke together in Yiddish and traded tales about life in Europe before the Holocaust. They raised money for Israeli charities. They celebrated birthdays and mourned deaths.

Christians, it seems to me, have the resources to organize their communal lives, and in particular the lives of elderly Christians, in a similar way. Community is, of course, central to Christianity at every life stage—after all, the very life of the Triune God tells us that we are persons only when we are in communion with one another. But community is especially important at certain life stages. Consider teenagers. Adolescence is all about the articulation of identity, and parents who want to form their teenagers will see to it that they are in communities—schools, churches, families, friend-ships—that can do the work of reminding them who they are.

So too with the elderly. When our memories fail, it is our community that can tell us who we are. If, like both of my grandmothers, we are lucky enough to have lived in the same town our whole adult lives, the community can remember our personal specific life histories. But even if we pick up and move across the country to be near our kids or to retire somewhere

sunny and warm, the community of the church can remind us
of our identity in Christ.

Scripture suggests that memory happens in community.
When Israel requires something of God, the people of Israel
remind God of their relationship, telling and retelling Him
stories of the promises He made to Israel, the things He did
for His people in past generations. As Kathleen Fischer has
explained, faith communities add "an essential dimension to
our remembering. In faith we not only gather our memories;
we recollect our lives before God. Our stories then take on . . .
meaning as a part of a larger story that redeems and embraces
them."

Griff's grandfather, Granddaddy Gatewood, will tell you that
his wife, who died a few years ago, was a beautiful woman, but
he does not remember many of the details of their life together,
or even of his life last week.

This loss of memory is, of course, hard and sad and bitter
for everyone who knows him. But it is eased a bit because Dr.
Gatewood lives in a community that remembers for him, that
can tell the stories of being Dr. Gatewood that even the man
himself has forgotten.

A few years ago, Dr. Gatewood told Griff that he loved
a woman I'll call Miss B., who has the funkiest glasses in the
South, and whom he has known forever, though he cannot
recall her name. One might, in a bittersweet sort of way, laugh
and wonder at that romantic claim—I did, when Griff told me
the story. I wondered how someone could be in love with a
woman whose name he could not remember.

But when I went to Americus and saw Dr. Gatewood and Miss B. together, his love for her made sense. Miss B., I'm sure, is interesting and charming in her own right, but she is also a part of the community that remembers Dr. Gatewood, and she remembers many of the things he would remember if he could. His love for her makes sense because it is a love played out against this backdrop: They have loved the same things and people their whole adult lives, and Miss B. remembers who Dr. Gatewood is.

---

**IN A 1990 SERMON** called "God Is a Woman, and She Is Growing Older," Rabbi Margaret Moers Wenig likened God to a grandmother. The process of repenting, Rabbi Wenig suggested, is a bit like going to visit the grandmother you've been neglecting. God, Rabbi Wenig wrote, "moves more slowly now. She cannot stand erect. Her hair is thinning. Her face is lined. Her smile is no longer innocent. Her voice is scratchy. Her eyes tire. Sometimes she has to strain to hear. Yet she remembers everything. . . . We are growing older, as God is growing older. How much like God we have become. For us, as well as for God, growing older means facing death. Of course, God will never die but she has buried more dear ones than we shall ever love. In God we see, 'tis a holy thing to love what death can touch. Like her, we may be holy, loving what death can touch, including ourselves, our own aging selves."

How do you feel when you imagine God aging? If the image feels uncomfortable, why? If you sit with or pray with the image, do you discover something about yourself, or about God, in the very discomfort?

---

∽

Contemporary America has done a pretty good job of marking some of the happier milestones of aging. We throw champagned and smiling parties for our parents' golden wedding anniversaries, and we roast our colleagues when they retire. What we have failed to mark are the harder places of aging—the day you sell your house and move into a retirement apartment or nursing home, the day you finally turn in your driver's license, the day you buy a wheelchair.

A few weeks ago, Lucy and I went to purchase, finally, a hearing aid for her old and imperfect ears. I had tried to come up with some ritual to mark this moment, but everything I could think of seemed hokey and contrived. (For example, I considered making a grand lunch of delicious cream sauce over orecchiette, the pasta whose name translates as "little ears.") In the end, we skipped the pasta and, after procuring the hearing aid, went to Continental Divide for margaritas instead. We toasted Giovanni Battista Porta, the sixteenth-century Neapolitan chemist and alchemist often credited with inventing the hearing aid.

Days later I ask Lucy whether she's adjusted to her new contraption. She says she's thrilled with it. "I can hear all sorts of details that had been lost in an indistinct buzz and mush," she says, but she also says that for an hour every morning, she turns her hearing aid off. "This is like closing your eyes when you pray," she says. "To help yourself concentrate in prayer, you close your eyes and render yourself temporarily blind, but only those of us with lousy hearing and top-of-the-line hearing aids have the option of temporarily rendering ourselves deaf." She says that in the silence, or buzz, or mush, worldly noises do not distract her from the clear voice of God.

# Discussion Questions

**1.** I mention, at the start of this chapter, a *midrash* about Abraham's request to appear older than his son:

> "Until Abraham there was no old age, so that one who wished to speak with Abraham might mistakenly find himself speaking with Isaac, or one who wished to speak with Isaac might mistakenly find himself speaking with Abraham. But when Abraham came, he pleaded for old age, saying, 'Master of the Universe, You must make a visible difference between father and son, between a youth and an old man, so that the old man may be honored by the youth.' God replied, 'As you live, I shall begin with you.' So Abraham went off, passed the night, and arose in the morning. When he arose he saw that the hair on his head and of his beard had turned white. He said, 'Master of the Universe, if You have given me white hair as a sign of old age, I do not find it attractive.' 'On the contrary,' God replied, 'the hoary head is a crown of glory' (Prov. 16:31)."

What is your response to Abraham's response to God? Why do you think Abraham struggled with the change he saw in himself?

How, according to this story, does God view physical signs of aging?

Now, read the second half of the Proverbs verse that is included in this story:

"Gray hair is a crown of glory; it is gained in a righteous life" (Prov. 16:31).

How might this full verse, and this *midrash,* instruct us in taking God's view of aging rather than our own? What do you think God's view of aging is?

**2.** I write that "The spirituality of aging inevitably involves preparing for one's death" (page 126). Athanasius of Alexandria, a fourth-century bishop, writes of viewing the length of one's life in light of eternity:

Let everyone above all have this zeal in common so that having made a beginning they not hesitate or grow fainthearted in their labors or say, "We have spent a long time in ascetic discipline." Instead, as though we were beginning anew each day, let each of us increase in fervor. For the entire lifetime of a human being is very brief when measured against the age to come; accordingly, all our time here is nothing compared with life eternal. Everything in the world is sold according to its value and things of equal value are exchanged, but the promise of eternal life is purchased for very little. For it is written, "The days of our life are seventy years or, if we are strong, perhaps eighty; more than this is pain and suffering." When we persevere in ascetic discipline for all eighty or even one hundred years, we will not reign for the equivalent of those one hundred years. Instead of a hundred years, we will reign forever and ever. And although we are contested on earth, we will not receive our inheritance here; we have promises in heaven instead. Once more: when we lay aside this perishable body we receive it back imperishable.

When you place aging in the context of eternity, what do you see? How does aging prepare us—and those we love—for eternity?

**3.** What does the slow progress of aging teach us about the importance of preparing for death? If God is one that honors the aged, what does this particular season of life have to teach us about preparing for eternity? What opportunities does the soul have in old age that it does not have in other seasons of life?

**4.** In Psalm 71, the psalmist writes: "Do not cast me off in the time of old age; do not forsake me when my strength is spent. . . . So even to old age and gray hairs, O God, do not forsake me, until I proclaim your might to all the generations to come." (Ps. 71:9, 18)

What do the psalmist's words portray about his fears regarding old age? Do any of the writer's fears resonate with yours? What is the desire of the psalmist? What are your desires for your life as you age? How might this psalm shape or reconfigure your thoughts and feelings about aging?

# NINE

# Hadlakat nerot

## Candle-lighting

I usually pooh-pooh anything that seems too trendy, but lately I've been filling my house with candles. Shaped like stars, crescents, or old-fashioned columns; blue, yellow, cranberry, glittery, striped; and of course scented: Jumping Jasmine and Lemonberry Meringue are my two most recent purchases, not to mention the Christmas Cookiedough candles I procured back in December.

I'm not alone in my candle fetish. "Candles [are] everywhere," an article in the *Miami Herald* declared, "and I mean *everywhere.*" Americans, apparently, spend more than two billion dollars a year on candles. And what is one of the

---

**"IT IS DIFFICULT TO IMAGINE** a more primal ritual than the lighting a candle," write rabbis Lawrence Kushner and Nehemia Polen. "The flame of a candle strikes us . . . as a perfect metaphor for a soul . . . yearning [for] its source on high." What spiritual metaphor do you see in a lit candle?

---

**"AS A CEREMONIAL OBJECT OR ART**, the candle is generally overlooked, yet it has great significance. Whether intended for practical purposes such as providing light, or for more evocative, quasi-magical ends, such as rekindling the winter sun, almost every festival and celebration incorporates the use of candles at some point. Fire is universally recognized as one of the basic elements of the world. It is mysterious, frightening, mesmerizing. Its attraction is almost irresistible. In the Kabbalah [Jewish mystical teaching], the image of a multicolored flame emanating from a candle is taken as a metaphor for God's relation to the world and man. The flame is a single entity, yet it appears to be undergoing constant change. The flame adheres to, relies on, and appears to emanate from the candle, yet is a distinct and separate entity. The white interior of the flame is constant, but its exterior is always in motion and changes color. Reducing fire to a few metaphors, however, robs it of its natural power and mystique. Fortunately the tradition, by incorporating the lighting of candles into the celebratory cycle in a number of different ways, left open the possibilities for recognizing the many potentialities of fire. It is for us to rediscover those potentialities and allow them to 'illumine our eyes.'"

— *THE FIRST JEWISH CATALOG:*
*A DO-IT-YOURSELF KIT*

**"ALWAYS LIGHT** a special candle for yourself when you pray, as it is said [in Is. 24:15], "'with lights, glorify God.'"
—From the Jewish work of ethics,
*Beit Middot*

hottest spots of the candlestick trade? Spirituality sales. Candles are part of bedside altars, sun-porch shrines, and meditation gardens. We sniff up all those scents not because we like aroma, but because we like aromatherapy. We are buying candles not just because of the romance they promise, but because they are good for the soul.

Even though—or perhaps because—literal illumination is as easy as, well, the flip of a switch, there's something remarkable about a candle. There seems to be no surer way to sacralize time or space than lighting a candle, and no quieter quiet than the silence of candlelight. Candles are peaceful, and transfixing, and also ancient. The candle craze may be recent, but New Agers aren't the first to figure out that candles can calm and still and center and sanctify. Candle making as we know it didn't begin until the twelfth century.

So candles per se are not found in Hebrew Scripture—the ancient children of Israel first spoke of oil lamps and torches, and only eventually adopted paraffin and palm oil and tallow. Candles are everywhere in contemporary Judaism. In the synagogue, in front of the cabinet that holds the Torah scrolls, burns the *ner tamid*, the eternal light, which is never allowed

**"ON SHABBAT**, the observant Jew is given an extra
soul, a Neshama Yeterah that descends from the tree
of life. This ancillary soul enables a person to 'celebrate
with great joy, and even to eat more than he is capable
of during the week.' The Shabbat candles represent
this spirit, and the woman of the house draws the flame
toward her eyes three times to absorb the light."

—BRENDA MILLER

to be extinguished. Memorial candles commemorate the dead. Chanukah is marked by the nightly lighting of an eight-branched candelabrum, the *menorah*.

And candles bracket the Jewish Sabbath. On Friday evening, women usher the Sabbath into their homes by lighting two candles. This is the moment when the hectic, last-minute Shabbat preparations become last week's work, and the peace of the Sabbath begins. After you light the candles, you close your eyes and beckon the light toward you three times with your hands, almost like you are drawing water from a basin to your face. There is something both meditative and practical about drawing the candlelight and the Sabbath stillness into yourself with your hands.

Candles mark the end of the Sabbath as well. In the ceremony called *havdalah*—which literally means "separation," in this case the separation between Sabbath and week—one lights a multi-wicked, braided candle. The sages explain the origins of the *havdalah* candle with a story. Adam was frightened at the end of the first Shabbat, and God gave him the flickering *havdalah* candle as a promise that Shabbat would return.

And each week, the confidence of the *havdalah* candle helps the transition from Sabbath to week; at the end of Shabbat, as the busyness of the work week begins, there is something reassuring in that last tranquil moment of candlelight. This promised quiet is part of what I am looking for when I light my Lemonberry Meringue and set it on the edge of my bathtub. Candles seem to create peace. You don't find candles lit in frenetic houses; you find them lit in houses where people are trying to pay attention.

Christian homes are not typically as candle-filled as Jewish homes. We Christians do not traditionally light candles to usher in the Sabbath or memorialize the dead. But in our communal home, the church, we do indeed have candles, at almost every turn of the liturgical year. We begin during Advent, the month before Christmas, during which we prepare to celebrate both Jesus' coming to earth in Bethlehem and His coming again in glory. We make Advent wreaths out of seasonal greens and four candles. Each week we light one more candle, edging closer out of the darkness of unredemption and toward the light of Jesus' coming.

This is, historically, a church ritual, but more and more people are making Advent wreaths for their homes, too. My five-year-old friend Henry insisted last year that his mother make an Advent wreath. When she asked why he wanted one so very much, he said he wanted something like Chanukah.

---

**"ALL THE DARKNESS** cannot extinguish the light of a single candle, yet one candle can illuminate all the darkness."

—ANCIENT JEWISH TEACHING

---

**"THE SPIRIT** of man is the candle of the Lᴏʀᴅ."

—Pʀᴏᴠᴇʀʙs 20:27ᴀ (ᴋᴊᴠ)

(A strange cultural reversal in a country that has so long been home to Jewish children wanting something like Christmas.) Griff, my beau, made an Advent wreath this year out of greens he plucked from a friend's yard. We put the wreath on his kitchen table and lit the candles before dinner, the wreath both making a candlelit date out of an ordinary meal and helping us live into a liturgical season so easily overshadowed by Santa Claus lists and shopping trips and cookie exchanges.

Advent and Christmas, in their wintery dark, are not the only liturgical moments for candles. The Advent wreath is really something of a dress rehearsal for the Paschal, or Easter, candle. In the Paschal candle, which Christians have been lighting since at least the sixth century, we see that candlelight symbolizes not only, as at Advent, Christ's Incarnation, but also His Resurrection. Here the flame points to the light of Christ's Resurrection triumphing over the darkness of death. The candle is lit in the dark of the nighttime Easter Vigil, and as it is processed through the church, the people sing this simple chant: "The light of Christ. Thanks be to God."

There is a story in the Talmud about Rabbi Jose. Rabbi Jose says he had studied and studied but was never able to understand a particular verse in Deuteronomy 28: "And you shall grope at noonday as the blind man gropes in pitch-black darkness." *Why,* Rabbi Jose wondered, *would a blind man grope specifically in the darkness? What difference does it make to him whether it is dark or light?* While musing on this problem one (pitch-black)

**"BLESSED** is the match, consumed in kindling flame.
Blessed is the flame that burns in the heart's secret places.
Blessed is the heart that knows, for honor's sake,
to stop its beating.
Blessed is the match, consumed in kindling flame."
—HANNAH SENESH

night, Rabbi Jose came across a blind man walking with a torch. "Why," Rabbi Jose asked the man, "do you carry that torch? With or without it, you cannot see a thing!" "True enough," said the blind man, "but as long as I carry this torch, other people can see me."

Rabbi Michael Strassfeld tells that story when teaching about Chanukah. The light of the *menorah,* he says, "lets us see each other and thereby enables us to help each other on our journeys. Despite the darkness, in [the Chanukah candles'] light we can see clearly from one end of [the] world to the other."

Rabbi Strassfeld, of course, is not speaking to the church, but I find in his words a helpful insight into one of Christendom's

**JEWISH LITURGIST** Penina V. Adelman suggests closing your eyes and pondering the following meditation when lighting a candle: "Think of a dark time in your own life. What was the light that brought you through this period? What inspired you to leave the darkness behind?"

**RABBI ZALMAN SCHACTER-SHALOMI** suggests
another candle meditation: "The aura of a candle defines
a sacred space; the lifespan of that flame defines a sacred
time. Light the candle and then bring the light into yourself.
. . . Close your eyes and then see it burning in your heart,
and then send out your prayer, your aspiration.

> Let your attention be the wick—
> your dedication the fuel—
> your soul the flame—
> rising and falling, rising and falling, reaching for that
> presence."

most persistent metaphors for Jesus: He is, we say, the light of
the world. He is the way, to borrow Rabbi Strassfeld's phrase,
that we can see clearly from one end of the world to the other.

In Judaism, candle-lighting has historically been associated
with women. (The *Miami Herald* article suggests that nothing
has changed: "Candles have failed to cross the gender gap.
They're a chick thing.") The Talmud names kindling the
Sabbath lights as one of three commandments specifically
incumbent upon women—the other two are baking *challah*
and observing the laws that govern sexual relations between
husband and wife.

Kindling is not all women do with candles. There is an old
Jewish folk custom called "the laying of wicks," observed during
the autumnal season of Rosh Hashanah and Yom Kippur (the

**ANOTHER POSSIBILITY** for candle meditation is this verse from the Gospel of John: "The light shines in the darkness and the darkness did not overcome it" (Jn. 1:5). Take a few moments before a lit candle—perhaps in a dark, nighttime room—and try to receive John's word. Perhaps picture Jesus there with you. *The light shines in the darkness and the darkness did not overcome it.*

new year and the Day of Atonement). Sometime during this holy season, women walked through cemeteries, measuring the gravestones with candlewick and reciting special prayers. On the night before Yom Kippur, they made candles from these wicks, Shabbat candles to be lit by those still living and memorial candles to be lit in honor of those who were dead. The candles, once made and lighted, were thought to awaken the dead, who would in turn intercede with God on behalf of the living. One famous prayer for the laying of wicks calls upon Adam and Eve to "rectify the sin by which they brought death to the world."

This is a somewhat obscure practice, to be sure, but one year in a fit of enthusiasm for the esoteric, my friend Shelby and I decided to head to a graveyard and measure some graves. It was only just past Yom Kippur, and Shelby had just read a scholarly article about the history of the laying of wicks. It seemed a good activity for two Jewish college girls. We pulled on rubber boots and packed raisins and other snacks and set off with our prayers and our lengths of candlewick. Once we got there, we didn't do much measuring. ("Did your article explain how exactly to do this measuring?" I asked Shelby. "Not really," she allowed.) But

**"AFTERWARDS, THIS HOLY PERSON** saw our dear
Lady holding a beautiful candle in her hand, and it burned
so beautifully that its light shone throughout the whole
world; and all round and round the candle the Name
of Jesus was written. Then our dear Lady said to this
person:—Behold, this burning candle signifies the Name
of Jesus, because He in very truth illuminates the hearts of
all who receive His Name with devotion, and pay it honour,
and bear it lovingly about with them."
—THE LIFE OF BLESSED HENRY SUSO

we did say the prayers, and we did eat our raisins, and Shelby told
me about her grandmother, who was buried in that very cemetery.
We never made the candles, either; eventually Shelby braided
the wick into thick, ropey jewelry, reminiscent of the bracelets
teenaged girls make at summer camp.

Shelby has since entered rabbinical school, and one autumn
weekend I go visit her in New York. We decide, finally, to
make some candles. When our great-grandmothers made them
on the frontier, the task must have been simpler; Shelby lists
all the necessary implements, and I know they did not have all
this stuff in the Nebraska territory in the nineteenth century:
scissors and a hammer and a jiffy wicker (I do not know what
this is) and a dash of Kemamide (ditto) and wax, of course, and
a candle mold. I am intimidated. This is perhaps not worth the
effort. Perhaps I should take myself down to Ye Olde Candle
Shoppe and purchase one of those brown candles with coffee
beans stuck (glued? Kemamided?) onto the side. But we get
started. Shelby lends me her wicking needle, and tells me that

## THE DAY IS O'ER,

My soul longs sore
For that eternal Morrow,
Which at length shall set us free
From all earthly sorrow.

Now it is night;
Christ, let Thy Light
Sin's darkness henceforth banish;
As God's candle in my breast,
Cause all gloom to vanish.

— A hymn by Johann Anastasius
Freylinghausen, translated by
Frances E. Cox.

The hymn is based on Isaiah 60:20 ("[T]he Lord will be your
everlasting light, and your days of mourning shall be ended").

Kemamide is a powder that helps candles come loose from their molds. ("Think bundt cakes," she says. "Kemamide is like the grease that prevents the cake from sticking in clumps on the inside of the pan.")

We melt the wax, and prepare the wick, and thread said wick through the mold, and at the end we have a candle. Eight of them, actually. I take them home. I light them at my bathroom sink, and at the kitchen counter, and on the old green desk, and by my bed. I like to keep them lit whenever I am home. Even when I am just lighting two thin tapers over dinner, I like to think about the light of Christ rectifying the sin by which came death to the world. *The Light of Christ,* I sometimes say to myself. *Thanks be to God.*

# Discussion Questions

**1.** Poet and teacher Yiskah Rosenfeld has written that candle-lighting bespeaks "creativity and completion" and "has a particularly physical, almost visceral component, marking space." Candle-lighting is also a way of marking time. To light Sabbath candles, writes Rosenfeld, is to touch "the power of transformation—turning ordinary time into sacred time." More mundanely, but just as urgent, "The kindling of the Sabbath candles might be a moment to think about carving out a time of rest in our over-committed schedules." Do you experience candle-lighting in any of these ways?

**2.** Consider this passage from Exodus: "You shall further command the Israelites to bring you pure oil of beaten olives for the light, so that a lamp may be set up to burn regularly. In the tent of meeting, outside the curtain that is before the covenant, Aaron and his sons shall tend it from evening to morning before the LORD. It shall be a perpetual ordinance to be observed throughout their generations by the Israelites."

Why do you think God commanded the people to have a light perpetually burning in the place where God's presence dwelt?

What is it about candlelight—in this case, lamplight—that points to something mysterious and holy?

**3.** I mention in this chapter that "You don't find candles lit in frenetic houses; you find them lit in houses where people are trying to pay attention" (page 141). What does the act of lighting a candle do that flipping a switch does not? How could the simple act of purposefully lighting a candle help us to slow down and attend to life in a different way? How can it potentially help us attend to God in a different way than we usually do?

**4.** In the Gospel of John, Jesus uses the language of light and lamps to explain who He and His followers are: "I am the light of the world. Whoever follows me will never walk in darkness but will have the light of life" (Jn. 8:12).

What do you think Jesus means when He refers to Himself as "the light of the world?" What is He saying about Himself?

∽

**5.** In the Book of Revelation, the seven churches that are mentioned in the Scripture are referred to as "lampstands" (Rev. 1:20). Oecumenius (the sixth-century author of the earliest existing Greek commentary on Revelation) wrote: "As he himself will explain a little later, the seven lampstands are the seven churches to which he is commanded to write. He calls them 'lampstands' since they carry in themselves the 'illumination of the glory of Christ.' He did not call them 'lamps' but 'lampstands,' for a lampstand itself does not possess the capacity to shine, but it bears that which is capable of illumination. Likewise, Christ mentally illuminates his churches. For just as the holy apostle exhorts those who have received the Faith, 'be as lights in the world, holding fast the word of life'—for indeed the lamp does not in itself possess light, but it is receptive of that light which comes to it—so also here the Evangelist saw the churches as lampstands and not as lights. For it is said concerning Christ, 'You shine forth marvelously from the everlasting mountains,' probably meaning the angelic powers; and again he says to the Father, 'Send out your light and your truth'; and again, 'the light of your countenance, O Lord.' And so, those who partake of the divine light are described on the one hand as lights and on the other hand as lampstands. He says that the lampstands are 'golden' on account of the value and excellence of those made worthy to receive the divine light."

What, according to Oecumenius, is the difference between a lampstand and a lamp? We do not have the ability to possess light on our own, but we can be receptive of the light that is given to us, from Christ. How might we be more receptive to Christ in our lives? How can the tangible act of lighting a candle remind us to allow the light of Christ to illuminate our own lives so that we might pass that light along to others?

**6.** At the end of the Sabbath, Jews ease their journey from Sabbath time back to week time with a short ceremony, called Havdalah. The ceremony is replete with wine, candle, and fragrant spices. Here is one of the blessings that is said when lighting the Havdalah candle to mark the end of Shabbat:

> Blessed are You, God, our Lord, King of the universe, who separates between the holy and the profane; between the light and dark; between Israel and the other nations; between the seventh day and the six days of the week. Blessed are You, God, who separates between the holy and the profane.

Rabbi Kerry M. Olitzky notes that this blessing "reads more like an affirmation of faith than a prayer, as if to say, 'With the extinguishing of this candle, we leave the holy, the sacred, and reenter the everyday, the mundane, the ordinary—with a renewed sense of optimism and purpose.'"

How might you incorporate this sort of holy intention and faith affirmation into the rhythm of your week—perhaps on Sunday evening?

# TEN

# Kiddushin

### Weddings

It is not rare, when you're in your mid-twenties, to be invited to three weddings in a single weekend. This weekend was one of those. I'd already declined an invitation to the gala bash (881 closest friends on the invite list) in Denver, but the other two weddings were in New York, spaced such that I could attend them both. Couple A was married on Saturday on a horse farm just upstate. Couple B was married on Sunday at a hotel in Manhattan. Couple A was Episcopalian. Couple B was Jewish. Both weddings were beautiful. At both, I toasted my friends with champagne, and flirted with men I'd never met before, and danced to Tony Bennett songs. At both weddings, the attendants wore dresses the color of vegetables, and the brides wore tulle. At both, I cried.

And yet, the weddings could not have been more different.

I love the solemn dignity of Christian weddings. I love the wedding rite of the Book of Common Prayer. I love Thomas Cranmer's rhythmic and bawdy 1549 language: "With this ring, I thee wed, . . . with my body, I thee worship." I love it when Christian brides and grooms choose the old language and *pledge their troth,* even though I always have to go home and look up *troth* in the dictionary. (*Troth,* n., "one's pledged fidelity," so actually pledging one's troth is something of a redundancy.)

But Jewish weddings are wonderful in their overt, undeniable joy. At Jewish weddings, everyone sings and dances and is almost raucous. My friend Shelby once remarked that Jewish weddings are just more fun than Christian weddings, and, on the whole, I have to agree.

The differences, though, are not merely aesthetic, Cranmer vs. klezmer or Hebrew instead of antique English. The ceremonies are different because the communities' understandings of marriage are different, and there is truth in each.

I admit that this is one of the places the Christian church has me forever: The way Christians make marriages makes sense to me. Christian wedding vows insist that marriage is a covenant, not a contract; that if marriage is not inviolable, divorce is still only to be undertaken in the rarest possible circumstances; that God is specially present at the Christian ceremony of marriage, and it is His presence that makes possible the astounding promises people promise; that marriage is, to use church-speak, sacramental.

Here is where Jewish and Christian theories of marriage conflict. The vows in a Jewish wedding ceremony are simple. As the groom puts the ring on the bride's finger, he says, "Behold, you are consecrated to me according to the laws of Moses and Israel." Then comes the reading of the *ketubah*, a contract dating at least to the second century CE. The traditional version names the date and place of the wedding, and then details the monetary settlement the groom will owe the bride in case of divorce. (In recent years, liberal Jews have written any number of alternate *ketubot*.) I remember, once upon a time, thinking this was a very

**WHEN I OFFICIATE** at a wedding, I follow the liturgy in the Book of Common Prayer. An important part of that prayer book's marriage service is the moment at which the officiant turns to the congregation and asks, "Will all of you witnessing these promises do all in your power to uphold these two persons in their marriage?" The people answer, "We will."

When you attend a wedding, do you see yourself as an integral part of the marriage that is taking place? Why or why not? Practically, how might you uphold two people in a marriage you witnessed?

grave but profound and insightful way to begin a marriage, this recognition of the possibility of failure. I now feel discomfited when sitting through this segment of Jewish weddings, when it is laid bare that I am indeed watching a contractual agreement, not a sacramental covenant; and I have to remind myself that Hebrew Scripture, the Old Testament, permits divorce under many circumstances. It is only with Jesus' stern words to the Pharisees that divorce became a very occasional exception to the ever more normative lifelong marriage.

In this nuptial particular, I feel that Christianity tells the best story. But theology, I realize, is different from sociology, and the statistics—which show evangelical Christians divorcing at a rate just slightly higher than that of the rest of America—suggest that however perfect in theory, something about Christian marriage-making (or, at least, Christian marriage-keeping) does not work. And here is where Jewish nuptials, depressing *ketubah*

**JESUS' FIRST RECORDED MIRACLE** in the New
Testament takes place at a wedding:

> On the third day there was a wedding in Cana of Galilee,
> and the mother of Jesus was there. Jesus and his
> disciples had also been invited to the wedding. When the
> wine gave out, the mother of Jesus said to him, "They
> have no wine." And Jesus said to her, "Woman, what
> concern is that to you and to me? My hour has not yet
> come." His mother said to the servants, "Do whatever he
> tells you." Now standing there were six stone water jars
> for the Jewish rites of purification, each holding twenty or
> thirty gallons. Jesus said to them, "Fill the jars with water."
> And they filled them up to the brim. He said to them,
> "Now draw some out, and take it to the chief steward."
> So they took it. When the steward tasted the water that
> had become wine, and did not know where it came from
> (though the servants who had drawn the water knew), the
> steward called the bridegroom and said to him, "Everyone
> serves the good wine first, and then the inferior wine after
> the guests have become drunk. But you have kept the
> good wine until now." Jesus did this, the first of his signs,
> in Cana of Galilee, and revealed his glory; and his disciples
> believed in him. (Jn. 2:1–11)

What meaning do you find in Jesus' first miracle in John
taking place at a wedding? What does this miracle say about
weddings, marriage, abundance, and celebration?

notwithstanding, are wise. If the *ketubah* makes my shoulders tense up, everything that surrounds the *ketubah* makes good sense. I wish we could import some of it to the church.

The visible symbols and icons of Jewish weddings are familiar. A Jewish couple is married under a *chuppah*, a four-cornered canopy, often made from cloth, sometimes extravagantly made of flowers. The *chuppah* symbolizes the roof of the home the couple will make together, and also the intimate fabric of their bedcovers, and also the sure protection of God's love.

Under the *chuppah*, after the exchange of rings and the reading of the *ketubah* and the pronouncing of blessings, comes the famous breaking of glass—the groom crushes a goblet (wrapped in a packet or bag, of course) under his feet. The broken glass warns of the frailty of marriage; it also recalls the destruction of the Temple in Jerusalem, a somber moment of Jewish history that should be remembered at even the most joyous occasions. Another interpretation holds that the loud crunch of the glass scares off any demons who might have been hanging around, plotting to trip up the wedding party. Still another holds that the breaking glass foreshadows the consummation of marriage.

Yet while the broken glass and the bold *chuppah* are memorable accoutrements of Jewish weddings, the most important things happen after, not under, the *chuppah*.

At the heart of weddings—because also at the heart of marriage—is the balance between privacy and community. Marriage, to be sure, is an intimate matter, the making of a partnership that knits two people together in secret and inside ways (just consider what Adam says of Eve: "bone of my bones and flesh of my flesh"). But it is a pernicious myth of modernity that marriage is merely private: Marriage is also a community endeavor. It is your friends and family who help you stay straight and true when your marriage feels too crooked or curvy. It is your sister or best friend or bridesmaid who can remind you why you ever married him in the first place. It is the neighbor or confidant who is just outside the thing who can sometimes tell you the truth about it.

This is the balance the Jewish wedding strikes exactly right. To see the balance, one must look at two end pieces of the Jewish wedding ceremony: *yichud* and *sheva brachot. Yichud* and *sheva brachot* both come after the ceremony—after the *chuppah* and the *ketubah* and the breaking of glass—but together they get at the essence of marriage-making.

*Yichud* is onomatopoeic. It is a hushed, whispered word, and it means "privacy." *Yichud*, privacy, is forbidden to the (Orthodox) Jewish couple before they are married. Until nuptials, the door must be kept open, there must be a chaperone—no sex, no impropriety, no aloneness. And so the very first thing he and she do after that glass is broken is escape off for a few minutes of *yichud*, a few minutes of aloneness, behind a closed door. In earlier eras, the marriage was actually consummated in the *yichud* room. Nowadays, there's just a good bit of smooching. If the couple is among the most devout Jews, those who observe the laws that require unmarried couples to have no physical contact at all, then there in the *yichud* room a single peck on the cheek is a spark-sending, faint-inducing big deal. I remember well the first Orthodox Jewish wedding I attended. When the bride and groom came out of the *yichud* room, they simply could not stop holding hands. It was the first time their hands had ever touched.

That coming out of the *yichud* room is the very point, the place where privacy gives way to community. As much as the hand-holding couple wanted to be alone, to stay immersed in alone for hours on end, they came back to their friends, to the neighbors and relatives who will uphold them in their new strange life together.

For observant Jews, there is no honeymoon, at least not immediately. The so-called "laws of family purity"—the laws that dictate when married couples may and may not have sex— require seven days of abstinence after The Wedding Night. And, really, what is the point of going on a honeymoon if you have to sleep in separate beds?

Instead of honeymooning, the newlyweds attend seven nights of parties in their honor. These parties are called the *sheva brachot*, after the "seven blessings" recited at each post-wedding bash. Intended to distract husband and wife from one another's sexual charms, these parties can range from a casual pizza get-together to the most formal champagne and caviar. (An added social plus: one can invite to the *sheva brachot* friends and acquaintances who didn't make it onto the wedding guest list.)

---

**CONSIDER THIS WORD** about the wedding at Cana by Theodore of Mopsuestia, a bishop who lived in the fourth and fifth centuries: "According to the will of the one who gave the command, the water was changed into wine, slaking the thirst of those who drank but also providing wine more abundantly for the couple's future."

What do you think Theodore means when he says that Christ was "providing wine more abundantly for the couple's future?"

---

Whether or not these fetes work as anti-aphrodisiacs is anyone's guess. What they do—not unlike the rites after a funeral—is push married couples into their community. Marriage, after all, is not just a change in individual circumstances. The new husband and wife will relate differently to one another, to be sure, but they will also engage the community differently, and night after night of festivities smooth that strange transition for everyone involved. Here are the *sheva brachot*, seven nightly reminders that marriage is a group project, a communal commitment.

✑

The great surprise of the week (at least, I am letting him think it was a surprise) is that Griff asked me to marry him. So now I find that all my theoretical musings about weddings suddenly become less theoretical.

I am already amazed at all the details, and how everyone has an opinion about which caterers I should call, and how easy it is to forget about marriage and think only about the wedding.

So far, I've gotten one piece of wedding advice that seems very sound. Our friends the Willards told us to pick one priority, one thing that we care about, and make that one thing as perfect as possible, and let everything else fall into place behind it. The photography? The reception venue? The dress?

I was assured I was marrying the right person when Griff said, without missing a beat, that the most important thing to him was somehow creating community at our wedding. (Where did he learn that, I wonder, since he didn't grow up Jewish?)

And so that is what we are trying to do. We are trying to invite people who are part of our pasts and presents. We will

**CHRISTIAN VOWS POINT**—implicitly and explicitly—to the presence of Christ in the wedding ceremony. Consider the following poem from ancient Syrian wedding liturgy, reflecting on the wedding rings:

"How many mysteries are hidden in the
Splendor of the wedding rings!
Our Lord Jesus Christ who is betrothed to
the Church and who, through His blood,
has established a dowry for her, has forged
her a ring with the nails of His crucifixion."

What do you think of this imagery—this idea that Christ has wedded himself to His Church by "forging" a ring out of the nails of His crucifixion? How did Christ's death enable Him to wed Himself to his Church? How might this image of the nails being bent into a wedding ring point ever more deeply to the "splendor" of the wedding rings— the "splendor" of marriage itself?

plan a weekend full of activities where our friends from the far-flung corners of the globe can, at least a little bit, get to know one another. And then, if we manage not to split up over questions of menu and music and boutonnières, we will one evening, some months from now, stand at the front of Christ Church while our priest asks our gathered community "Will all of you witnessing these promises do all in your power to uphold these two persons in their marriage?" And our community will answer, "We will."

# Discussion Questions

**1.** Consider this Jewish nuptial blessing: "Bestow abundant joy to this beloved couple as you bestowed joy to the first man and wife in the Garden of Eden. Be praised, O Lord, who bestows joy on the groom and bride. Be praised, O Lord our God, King of the universe, who have created joy and gladness, a groom and his bride, mirth and exultation, dancing and jubilation, love and harmony, peace and companionship. O Lord our God, may there soon be heard again in the cities of Judah and the streets of Jerusalem, glad and joyous voices, the voices of groom and bride, the jubilant voices of those joined in marriage under the wedding canopy, the voices of young people feasting and singing. Be praised, O Lord our God, who causes the groom to rejoice with his bride."

What does this blessing imply about God's delight in marriage? What allusion do you see here to the presence of the community at the heart of the marriage?

**2.** Jesus tells a parable to His followers in the Book of Matthew that has to do with the guests at a wedding:

> Once more Jesus spoke to them in parables, saying: "The kingdom of heaven may be compared to a king who gave a wedding banquet for his son. He sent his slaves to call those who had been invited to the wedding banquet, but they would not come. Again he sent other slaves, saying, 'Tell those who have been invited: Look, I have prepared my dinner, my oxen and my fat calves have been slaughtered, and everything is ready; come to the wedding banquet.' But they made light of it and went away, one to his farm, another to his business, while the rest seized his slaves, mistreated them, and killed them. The king was enraged. He sent his troops, destroyed those murderers, and burned their city. Then he said to his slaves, 'The wedding is ready, but those invited were not worthy. Go therefore into the main streets, and invite everyone you find to the wedding banquet.' Those slaves went out into the streets and gathered all whom they found, both good and bad; so the wedding hall was filled with guests." (Matt. 22:1–10)

Why do you suppose the "king was enraged" when the invited guests "made light" of the invitation to the wedding banquet? What did their dismissal imply, both about the king and about the marriage itself? Why was this so problematic?

∽

**3.** When she recently preached on this passage at Duke Chapel, Barbara Brown Taylor offered this interesting interpretation:

> Everyone else at the banquet seems to have gotten a memo that the under-dressed guest has not. When the magnificent king approaches him, with anger still radiating from his royal person over his first, disastrously received effort at being generous, the under-dressed guest has no time to think, much less get the textbook. "Friend," the king says to him (a lousy translation; "buster" works much better). "Buster," the king says to him, "how did you get in here without a wedding garment?" Oh, God. It's one of *those* dreams.
>
> Why do I think it's a dream? Because real people don't turn down a king's dinner invitation, much less torture and kill the messengers who came to fetch them. Because once you have a whole ox and several fatted calves on serving platters, they won't keep while you wage war on a whole city, kill its inhabitants, and torch the place. Because who really expects someone nabbed in the middle of an oil change to have a clean wedding garment in the back of the truck?
>
> Jesus called it a parable, which is almost the same thing as a dream. It's not a once-and-for-all story. It's a story you can walk around in, a story that wants a response from you—hopes for a response from you— one that changes as you change, so that it is different the tenth time you hear it than it was at the first.

Matthew was certainly looking for a response, but his reasons for recording the story don't exhaust our reasons for entering it. The king, the banquet, the dress code, the failure—the exposure of the failure, the judgment, the free fall into outer darkness—you know this story, don't you?

You even know why it's no good to be a hypocrite. It really *is* deadly, to keep two yous going—the public you and the private you, the you you say you are and the you you act like, the you you dress like and the you you really are. You say you're an environmentalist but you gobble energy like a suburban mall. You say "have a blessed day" to the lady at the bank and then pull into traffic like a demon straight from hell. You tell everyone who will listen how worried you are about the public schools, about the people who are losing their homes, about the election, but you don't do anything about them. You say you will go to the vineyard but you don't.

Matthew seems to think that all this twoness is about gaining advantage over other people, but I think that's circumstantial. When he wrote his gospel, he was dealing with religious people who were living high on widow's mites, who were using their theological educations—their institutional privileges—to climb on top of other people. While that hypocrite's club still has plenty of members, Matthew stays so busy with them that he seems to lose sight of the people whose twoness has less to do with their inflated sense of their own worth than with their terrible fear that they are worth nothing at all.

It's just as deadly, this other hypocrisy. You look all pulled together but you are really a wreck. You make a good salary but you're on welfare in your heart. You can speak three languages. You have a college degree. You know which fork to use, and still you keep waiting for someone to come and arrest you—to ask you how you got in here—and when you cannot get a single word to pass your lips because you have been found out at last—you hold out your hands so the usher will have an easier time binding them. You're scared of the outer darkness but it's no surprise, really. It is where you always feared you belonged.

Based on personal experience, I would have to say that the only thing worse than the twoness is waiting for someone to find out about it. The only thing worse than showing up in your dream with the wrong clothes on—no clothes on?—is waiting for someone to notice. Then someone does, and while there can be real terror in that moment—especially if the noticer happens to be a really mad king—there can also be real relief in that moment—because someone finally noticed your twoness and now you don't have to pretend anymore. Someone was not fooled by your pretense. Someone has reached past the two yous to tap the real you on the shoulder, and even if he calls you "Buster," the jig is up.

Here's the good news: because your twoness has been exposed, your wholeness is a real possibility, perhaps for the first time. Because someone has paid attention to you long enough to notice what it was about you that didn't fit—someone who has decided not to let you pass this time, who has the regal nerve to walk right up to you and say, "Which one's the lie? This isn't a Halloween party. Take off the mask."

Well. Now that that's happened, you have a chance to be made new. When this dream comes back, you're going to play it differently—because you can, now. When that king approaches you next time, you're going to let him know you got the point.

How do you respond to Taylor's interpretation of Jesus' famous wedding parable? Does it make sense to you to see what happened in this way?

# ELEVEN

# Mezuzot

### Doorposts

When I was twelve, a friend from the synagogue gave me a *mezuzah*: a small roll of parchment tucked inside a glass tube. The glass was gauzy, like translucent Tiffany glass, streaked with summer colors: pink, and green, and purple. At the top and bottom of the tube, there were tiny holes made for tiny nails, and I took the mezuzah home, and said the blessing that praises the God who has commanded us to affix the *mezuzah*, and nailed it to the doorframe outside my bedroom.

The practice of affixing a *mezuzah* to one's door finds it's origin in a passage from Deuteronomy: "You shall love the Lord your God with all your heart and with all your soul and with all your might. These words, which I am commanding you today, shall be on your heart. . . . You shall write them on the doorposts of your house and on your gates."

*You shall write them on the doorposts of your house:* In obedience to that verse, Jews purchase special tiny scrolls of parchment on which are calligraphied fifteen verses from the sixth and eleventh chapters of Deuteronomy (the very verses in which the command to *inscribe them on your doorposts* is found). The

**MARKING YOUR DOORWAY** with a *mezuzah*, or
something like it, as faithful Jews usually do, is not the
only way to mark your home as a place that welcomes
God. Scholars have considered at length the way
American Christians have, over the centuries, created
sacred space in their homes. Historian Colleen McDannell,
for example, argues that families' displaying their Bibles
(prominently, on specially constructed "marble and wood
brackets"), as well as decorated quotidian objects like
dishware with "Christian symbols, pious sayings, and
biblical figures," help sanctify the home. Look around your
home. What objects mark the space as a place where
God is welcome? What one thing might you like to change
in your kitchen, or in your bedroom, to help create zones
of sanctity in those rooms?

parchment is hidden inside a decorative case or tube. Both the
parchment itself and the plastic or ceramic or silver or wooden
case are called a *mezuzah* (the plural is *mezuzot*). These are the
boxes you see on the doors outside Jewish homes. You'll find
them inside, too, on the doorposts to any room in which people
live: bedrooms, kitchens, drawing rooms—every room, really,
other than bathrooms and stables.

In college (yes, one is commanded to hang a *mezuzah* on
one's college dorm room doorpost—anywhere one will be
living longer than a month), I purchased a new *mezuzah*. You

purchase the scroll itself, generally, at a Judaica shop, but you can find the cases anywhere. I bought mine, a small silver case with delicate filigree, at an art gallery in Greenwich Village.

Jews got serious about the business of decorating *mezuzah* cases in the eighteenth or nineteenth century. There is an elaborate North African *mezuzah* case that dates to sometime in the 1700s, and by the nineteenth century Jews in Russia, eastern Europe, and Morocco were shaping *mezuzah* cases out of silver, creating miniature arks and fish and other pretty symbols in which to house their slices of parchment. Today one can find *mezuzah* cases made of pewter, clay, wood, crystal, even hammered gold. Creative craftsy types can make their own *mezuzot*; outside my friend Perry's bedroom is a *mezuzah* made from a pink plastic toothbrush case.

The younger set can purchase a Snoopy *mezuzah*, a Braves *mezuzah* in the shape of a baseball bat, a dinosaur *mezuzah* painted in Barney-purple. The hard-nosed toy-shopper can find miniature *mezuzot* made for dollhouses. (I've even heard there are special tiny *mezuzot* for Barbie to use, but I've never seen one, nor do I recall reading that the WASPish Mattel doll converted to Judaism.)

Is consumer culture infecting the *mezuzah*? Sure. But there is something grand to the dressing up of the simple *mezuzah*—it is consonant with the underlying Jewish attitude toward beauty. One should, whenever possible, beautify one's commandments. Why have a plain Jane *mezuzah* when one can affix works of art to one's doorposts?

From Snoopy to silver filigree, almost every *mezuzah* case is decorated with the Hebrew letter *shin*: שׁ. This three-pronged letter, which looks a little like the top of a pitch-fork, begins the *Shema*, the Jewish prayer, found in Deuteronomy 6:4, that declares the oneness of God: *Hear, O Israel, the* LORD *our God, the* LORD *is one.* This prayer, repeated over and over in the Jewish liturgy, is meant to be the last thing a Jew says before dying. It is included in the verses copied onto the *mezuzah* parchment. The *mezuzah* case, then, is not just a decorative item. It is also a restatement of the essence of Jewish faith.

*Shin* is also the first letter of the word *shalom*, peace. If having a *mezuzah* on one's door does not necessarily make one's home a peaceful refuge from the hostile world, it does serve as a reminder: a reminder of *shalom bayit,* peace in the home, an ideal toward which every Jewish home is meant to strive. Once, when my college roomie and I were duking it out over the dishes (in the sink) and the bathtub (filthy) and the phone (ringing much too late at night), the *mezuzah* squelched our screaming. In the middle of railing about the long hair destined to clog our bathtub pipes, my roommate walked to our bedroom door and tapped on the front of the *mezuzah*, and we smiled and laughed and breathed deeply and started to wash the dishes. Little *mezuzah* reminders don't work miracles, of course, but sometimes they help the fights simmer down and the dishes get clean.

The *shin* that decorates a *mezuzah* case also stands for the phrase *Shomer daltot Yisrael*, "guardian of the doors of Israel." And, indeed, since at least the Middle Ages, many Jews have thought of the *mezuzah* as an amulet, a charm-working talisman that would keep the demons and evil spirits away. The rabbis have not been overly fond of that folk belief, but even they have allowed that a *mezuzah*, insofar as it is a small physical reminder of God's power and presence, does keep us from harm's way. According to the Talmud, the Jew who wears phylacteries on his arm and fringed *tzitzit* on his garments and affixes a *mezuzah* to his door, "is sure not to sin because he has many reminders of God; and these reminders are the very guardian angels who protect him from sinning."

Finally, the *shin* that decorates *mezuzah* cases is also the letter that begins the word *shofar*. A *shofar* is a ram's horn, and in synagogues, the *shofar* is blown like a trumpet during the most sacred days of the Jewish year, the High Holy Days of Rosh Hashanah and Yom Kippur, the new year and the Day of Atonement. The lowing song of the *shofar* is both a call to atone and a proclamation of faith. The *mezuzah*, too, which interrupts the smooth line of the doorframe and juts into your line of vision, is a proclamation. A *mezuzah*—like Chanukah *menorahs,* which Jews are enjoined not only to light, but to set in their windows—is a real, visible, public witness, a declaration to anyone who would walk by that this is a Jewish home. The people who live here are Jewish, and they are proud of it.

That proclamation is more noticeable here in Charlottesville than in New York. Manhattan is home to such a sizable Jewish community that after a while one doesn't really notice the *mezuzot*. In Charlottesville, a *mezuzah* is a rarer thing. My friend Vanessa lives on St. Anne's Lane, and I can never remember her house number, but whenever I go to visit, I know her house because the *mezuzah* marks it.

Perhaps the most startling Charlottesville *mezuzah* is that of Kevin Hechtkopf. Kevin is the president of Hillel (the campus Jewish organization) here at the University of Virginia, and he lives on the Lawn, the architectural and historical heart of the entire university. Kevin, now in his final year at UVA, had not bothered with *mezuzot* during his first three years of college. But an iridescent black *mezuzah* now hangs outside his room on the widely trafficked Lawn. Kevin's *mezuzah* is spied daily by professors, administrators, students, even sometimes a governor

**ABRAHAM P. BLOCH** offers some insight into the connection between the *mezuzah* and the idea of protection:

> The doorpost played an important part in several rituals. The blood of the paschal lamb was smeared on both doorposts (Exod. 12:7). The ear of a Hebrew slave who continued in servitude beyond seven years was pierced at the doorpost (Exod. 21:6). The doorpost was an appropriate spot from which to declare the unity of God (Deut. 6:4-9) and to proclaim the parental obligation to instruct children in the lessons of the Torah (Deut. 11:13-21). Before the introduction of parchments and cases, the foregoing two passages were most likely written directly on the doorposts. . . . The notion that a mezuzah is endowed with protective powers gained early credence. The belief probably stemmed from the biblical account of the smearing of the blood of the paschal lamb on the doorposts of Jewish homes, which granted Jews immunity from the tenth plague. "He will not suffer the destroyer to come in unto your houses" (Exod. 12:23).

or visiting dignitary. Here on the grounds of the college designed by the same Thomas Jefferson who drafted Virginia's Bill of Religious Toleration, Kevin's *mezuzah* is a proclamation. It says, in his words, that "you can be Jewish at UVA—you don't have to hide it."

&#x221d;

Years ago, I gave away my delicate silver and glass *mezuzot*. There are no Christian *mezuzot*; I don't even have a Christian fish pasted to the bumper of my car. I have filled my apartment with crosses and old church fans and Crucifixion scenes done in Indian batik. These objects decorate. Like churchly stained-glass windows, they tell stories. They help me remember. They are still not *mezuzot*, though. They do not always ask what I want a Christian home to be like. They do not proclaim to anyone who might pass by that this home is a Christian home.

About two years ago, my friend Bobby and I were walking up Broadway. We saw, on the sidewalk, an old door someone was discarding. "Hey look," I said, "there's a sign on this door." And, indeed, taped to the front of the lonesome sidewalk door was a sign the size of a postcard with a quotation from Psalm 121: "The Lord shall preserve thy going out and thy coming in from this time forth, and even for evermore." The small print on the bottom told me the sign had been produced by the Life-Study Fellowship in Noroton, Connecticut. Someone, perhaps the guy who was getting rid of the door, had scribbled on the sign *Keep home safe thank God*. The handwriting was shaky, that of a child or a ninety-year-old.

"Look at this sign," I said to Bobby, marveling.

"Do you want it?" Bobby asked.

"Why, yes, I do," I said. And I pried the little sign off the door and put it in my purse.

I used to keep it propped up on my dresser, mixed in with a photo of my father, a bakelite compact I bought on eBay, and an old wooden glove box that I keep full of forget-me-nots. While helping me clean for a party, my friend Molly said, "Lauren, why don't you put this sign up on your door?" *Good thinking,*

I thought. I took the sign and located a roll of tape and began to affix it to my bedroom door. "No," Molly said, "your front door."

I inhaled sharply. "But, Molly," I said, "if I do that, the whole world will know I'm a Christian." Molly looked at me and wiggled her eyebrows. There it was, my old discomfort with what we Christians call witnessing, my ever-present hesitation to proclaim the gospel, my deep-seated suspicion that Christianity is fine as long as it's private.

Molly cleared her throat. She tapped her fingers on the top of my dresser. "Hmmm," I said. (Did I mention this was a St. Lucia Day party, and that I'd spent all afternoon trying to make the cardamom-and saffron-filled St. Lucia Day buns, and that only Christian nerds newly infatuated with the saints' days do such things?) "Right," I said, and I went to the front door and taped up the small rectangular sign from the Life-Study Fellowship.

It is not quite a *mezuzah*. Hanging up a sign one found while waltzing down Broadway is not quite the same as fulfilling a no-nonsense commandment to inscribe the doorposts of your house. But this sign accomplishes some of the same space and memory work of *mezuzot*.

Every time I come home I see the sign, and I remember that I claim to actually believe in this God who will preserve my going out and coming in, and I remember that this home is supposed to be a Christian home. It is to be a home into which I invite strangers, and in which I organize my time through prayers, and in which I do work that might somehow infinitesimally advance the kingdom of God.

And when I walk in and out of my apartment and see the psalmist sign, I also remember the proclamation that I am making to others: the sign tells you that I am a person who is trying to be a Christian, and in telling that to you, I am inviting you to hold me to it.

It is just the doorway, but this is the beginning of making Christian space out of an ordinary apartment.

# Discussion Questions

**1.** At the beginning of this chapter, I refer to the verses in Deuteronomy in which the Jewish practice of putting *mezuzot* is grounded:

> Now this is the commandment—the statutes and the ordinances—that the LORD your God charged me to teach you to observe in the land that you are about to cross into and occupy, so that you and your children and your children's children may fear the LORD your God all the days of your life, and keep all his decrees and his commandments that I am commanding you, so that your days may be long. Hear therefore, O Israel, and observe them diligently, so that it may go well with you, and so that you may multiply greatly in a land flowing with milk and honey, as the LORD, the God of your ancestors, has promised you.
>
> Hear, O Israel: The LORD is our God, the LORD alone. You shall love the LORD your God with all your

heart, and with all your soul, and with all your might. Keep these words that I am commanding you today in your heart. Recite them to your children and talk about them when you are at home and when you are away, when you lie down and when you rise. Bind them as a sign on your hand, fix them as an emblem on your forehead, and write them on the doorposts of your house and on your gates. (Deut. 6:1–9)

Why do you think God wanted the people to "keep these words that I am commanding you today in your heart"? How would the practices of "reciting them to your children," "bind[ing] them as a sign on your hand," and "writ[ing] them on the doorposts of your house" help people keep these commandments in their hearts?

**2.** How do physical reminders of spiritual realities help keep us attentive to God? The *mezuzah* is, among other things, a way of marking one's home as a place where people encounter God. What are some ways that you could (or do) mark your home as sacred space?

**3.** Marian Nash, a convert to Judaism, explains the importance of the *mezuzah* in her life this way:

I walk my new husband, Jim, to the elevator and kiss him good-bye. The door closes and I whisper my prayer of thanks for him and for his return. I touch the mezuzah hung on the right side of our doorframe; I bring my fingers to my lips. To myself I say, Torah, and go into the kitchen for a glass of water. . . . I am most comfortable acknowledging the mezuzah when I am alone or with Jim. Visitors following me into the apartment may catch the swift movement of my hand reaching up, but I tend to hide the final act when my fingers go to my lips. I feel their curiosity at my back. I wish I weren't too self-conscious to turn to them and say, "I like how this leads me to contemplate how I will be in my home." But I am. . . . Many times Jim and I will be having a disagreement in the elevator going up to our apartment. I will be pit-bulling the topic, clamping my opinion and viewpoint down hard on Jim's every word and shaking it in the jaws of my righteousness. Reaching up to acknowledge the mezuzah on our doorway breaks the momentum. It gives me that split-second chance to lighten up and ask, Would I rather have some peace and quiet? The heated moment quickly cools, as I feel pressed to find a solution. . . . May the words of Torah, Lord our God, be sweet in our mouths and in the mouths of all Your people. . . . I impress the words of Torah on my heart to try to remember to be kind, forgiving, creative, and compassionate.

For Nash, touching the mezuzah is a spiritual practice that yields small but concrete fruit. How might you make the moment of entering your front door a real moment of transition, a moment when you pause and, to borrow Nash's phrasing, contemplate how you will be in your home?

# ACKNOWLEDGMENTS

## (2003 Edition)

I am grateful to those who read drafts of many of these chapters: Molly Bosscher Davis, Kristine Harmon, Charles Marsh, Jenny McBride, Erika Meitner, Vanessa Ochs, Professor Marvin R. Wilson, Felicia Wu Song, Beth Bogard Vander Wel, Brian Vander Wel, and my students at the Charlottesville Writing Center.

Special thanks to Griff Gatewood, who worked his way through many drafts, and who helped me keep body and soul together during a few hectic writing weeks; and to Shani Offen, old friend and peerless *dikduk* point girl; and to Mary E. Lyons, for sharp eyes and pencils, and hospitality. Amanda Beer, proprietor of Charlottesville's remarkable Splintered Light bookstore, provided encouragement and, of course, books.

Thanks to Carol Mann, heroic agent and confidante, and to the good folks at Paraclete, most especially Lil Copan, for patience and fortitude (and all the other virtues besides).

## (Study Edition)

Special thanks to Ann Swindell, for her heroic research for this new edition.

# NOTES

## Introduction to the Study Edition

p. ix. *"Fasting can heighten our sense of solidarity with the destitute and the hungry throughout the world"*
Samuel M. Stahl, "Maimonides' Discussion of Virtue," in *Shemonah Perakim: A Treatise on the Soul*, eds. and trans. Leonard S. Kravitz and Kerry M. Olitzky (New York: UAHC, 1999), 58.

pp. ix–x. *The Sabbath day is a soul for the other six days . . . to the six days of activity.*
Quoted in Elliot K. Ginsburg, *The Sabbath in the Classical Kabbalah* (Albany: State University of New York Press, 1989), 88.

p. xv. *Taste the goodness of your Redeemer . . . delight in swallowing.*
Quoted in Paul J. Griffiths, *Religious Reading: The Place of Reading in the Practice of Religion* (New York: Oxford University Press, 1999), 43.

## Introduction to the First Edition

p. xviii. *This* midrash *explains a curious turn of phrase in Exodus 24.*
Exodus 24:7 Talmud, Masechet Shabbat 88a.

p. xix. *Christian tradition has developed a wealth of practices. . . .*
The most influential recent book on Christian spiritual practice is Richard J. Foster, *Celebration of Discipline: The Path to Spiritual Growth* (San Francisco: Harper and Row, 1978).

p. xx. *"Christ, and him crucified."*
1 Corinthians 2:2.

## ONE: Shabbat/Sabbath

pp. 1–2. *"On Friday afternoon . . . Shabbat is a meditation of unbelievable beauty."*
Nan Fink, *Stranger in the Midst: A Memoir of Spiritual Discovery* (New York: Basic Books, 1997), 95–96.

p. 2. *The Sabbath is the dream of perfection . . . as if it were already redeemed.*
Quoted in Ginsburg, *The Sabbath in the Classical Kabbalah*, 93–94.

p. 3. *"Remember the Sabbath day and keep it holy."*
Exodus 20:8.

p. 3. "observe *the Sabbath day and keep it holy.*"
Deuteronomy 5:12.

p. 3. *"come to worship before me."*
Isaiah 66:23.

p. 3. *In the end, all will be Sabbath.*
Ginsburg, *The Sabbath in the Classical Kabbalah*, 72.

p. 4. *"You shall not . . . sojourner who stays with you."*
Exodus 20:10 and Deuteronomy 5:14.

p. 4. *With the Sabbath-soul . . . on high and below.*
Quoted in Ginsburg, *The Sabbath in the Classical Kabbalah*, 131.

p. 5. *"What happens . . . it is God's world."*
Lis Harris, *Holy Days: The World of a Hasidic Family* (New York: Touchstone Books, 1995), 68–69.

p. 6. *A 70 hour work week . . . God and humanity.*
Ellen F. Davis, "The Sabbath: The Culmination of Creation," *Living Pulpit* 7, no. 2 (1998): 6–7.

p. 8. *"Therefore do not let anyone judge you . . . the reality, however, is found in Christ."*
Col. 2: 16–17 NIV.

p. 8. *"the Sabbath was made for man, not man for the Sabbath."*
Mark 2:27 NIV.

p. 9. *"Six days shall you labor and do all your work. But the seventh day is a sabbath to the LORD your God."*
Exodus 20:9–10 and Deuteronomy 5:13–14.

p. 10. *"Good Sabbaths make good Christians."*
Dorothy Bass, "Keeping Sabbath," in Dorothy Bass, ed., *Practicing Our Faith: A Way of Life for a Searching People* (San Francisco: Jossey–Bass, 1997), 83–88.

p. 10. *"Under the New Testament . . . Retire to rest betimes."*
Johann Friedrich Starck, *Daily Handbook for Days of Joy and Sorrow*, excerpted in Peter C. Erb, *Pietists: Selected Writings* (New York: Paulist Press, 1983), 181–82.

p. 11. *"Here we find roughly parallel requirements . . . properly nourished and cared for."*
Norman Wirzba, *Living the Sabbath: Discovering the Rhythms of Rest and Delight* (Grand Rapids, MI: Brazos, 2006), 144–145.

p. 12. *"Sabbath, seventh day of creation . . . tired man and woman might prefer yes."*
Elizabeth Ehrlich, *Miriam's Kitchen: A Memoir* (New York: Penguin, 1998), 355.

p. 13. *"SIX DAYS YOU SHALL LABOR . . . SEEK THE FAVOR OF THE LORD"*
Quoted in *The Classic Midrash: Tannaitic Commentaries on the Bible*, trans. Reuven Hammer (Mahwah, NJ: Paulist, 1995), 159.

p. 14. *"Remember the Sabbath day continually . . . prepare it for use on the Sabbath."*
Quoted in Michael Katz and Gershon Schwartz, *Searching for Meaning in Midrash: Lessons for Everyday Living* (Philadelphia: Jewish Publication Society, 2002), 79.

p. 14. *"For Resh Lakis said . . . leaving him weakened and sad."*
From Ta'anit 27b,. *The Talmud: The Steinsaltz Edition*, ed. and trans. Rabbi Israel V. Berman, Vol. XIV, Part II (New York: Random House, 1995), 186.

p. 15. *"imposes a regular periodical holiday . . . here is the Spirit of God."*
From "Sermon 8.6" as quoted in Joseph T. Lienhard, ed. *Exodus, Leviticus, Numbers, Deuteronomy* (Downers Grove, IL: InterVarsity, 2001), 104.

## TWO: Kashrut/Fitting Food

p. 18. *"Kashrut is best understood . . . as a way of sanctifying a basic need."*
Anita Diamant, *The New Jewish Wedding Book, Revised Edition* (New York: Scribner's, 2001), 117.

p. 18. *"The main service of God is through eating . . . as with prayer."*
Jay Michaelson, *God in Your Body: Kabbalah, Mindfulness and Embodied Spiritual Practice* (Woodstock, VT: Jewish Lights, 2007), 3.

p. 18. *He suggests praying one line from Psalm 145 . . . try to know deeply that God has sustained all of it.*
Michaelson, *God in Your Body*, 14–15.

p. 19. *"Thou shalt not seethe a kid in his mother's milk."*
Deuteronomy 14:21 KJV.

p. 19. *No shellfish, no pork . . . now it is a meat pot forever.*
This list is inspired by Elizabeth Erlich's wonderful musings on keeping kosher: Elizabeth Erlich, *Miriam's Kitchen: A Memoir* (New York: Viking, 1997), 14–17.

p. 20. *Rabbi Abraham Joshua Heschel observed . . . death (meat) and life (milk).*
Arthur Waskow, *Down-to-Earth Judaism: Food, Money, Sex, and the Rest of Life* (New York: William Morrow, 1997), 78.

p. 21. *"Dovetailing with the broader local food movement . . . impact of our farming practices?"*
Andrea Lieber, *The Essential Guide to Jewish Prayer and Practices* (New York: Alpha Books, 2012), 260.

p. 22. *In the Book of Acts . . . "you must not call profane."*
Acts of the Apostles 10:13, 15.

p. 22. *God has given . . . all that God's people need to be able to be God's friends and to eat with him."*
Samuel Wells, *God's Companions: Reimagining Christian Ethics* (Malden, MA: Blackwell, 2006), 140, 197.

p. 23. *"[T]hrough observance of [Kashrut] . . . our selves and our bodies."*
Richard Siegal, Michael Strassfeld, and Sharon Strassfeld, *The First Jewish Catalog: A Do-It-Yourself Kit* (Philadelphia: The Jewish Publication Society, 1965), 18.

p. 23. *Humanity's first sin was disobedience manifested in a choice about eating.*
Waskow, *Down-to-Earth Judaism*, 17–21.

p. 24. *"By attending to the sources of our food and buying locally . . . in which we cater to our immediate wishes."*
David Grumett, "A Christian Diet: The Case for Food Rules," *Christian Century* 127, no. 7 (2010): 34–37.

pp. 25–26. *The second chapter of* The Supper of the Lamb *. . . "His present delight."*
Robert Farrar Capon, *The Supper of the Lamb: A Culinary Reflection* (New York: Pocket Books, 1970), 10–11, 15–16. I am grateful to the Reverend Brian Vander Wel for directing my attention to Capon's onion.

p. 27. *"[W]hen you eat . . . sweetness which is the life of the food."*
Michaelson, *God in Your Body*, 15.

pp. 26–27. *"Even if you walk or bike . . . some serious gas."*
Barbara Kingsolver, *Small Wonder* (New York: Harper Collins, 2002), 114. Thanks to Mary Lyons for pointing out to me that Edna Lewis and Alice Waters pioneered and popularized the current fascination with seasonal eating.

p. 28. *"'Eating is an agricultural act' . . . which is to say eating in ignorance, are fleeting."*
Michael Pollan, *The Omnivore's Dilemma: A Natural History of Four Meals* (New York: Penguin, 2006), 11.

pp. 33–36. *Since each of the injunctions is prefaced . . . confounds the general scheme of the world.*
Mary Douglas, "The Abominations of Leviticus," quoted in *Community, Identity, and Ideology: Social Scientific Approaches to the Hebrew Bible*, eds. Charles E. Carter and Carol L. Meyers (Winona Lake, IN: Eisenbrauns, 1996), 119–134. Reproduced by permission of Taylor & Francis Books UK.

pp. 36–37. *"About noon the next day . . . was suddenly taken up to heaven."*
Acts 10:9–16.

p. 37. *"Suppose you are tired and eat to regain the strength . . . such deeds drag you into hell."*
Rami Shapiro, *Tanya, the Masterpiece of Hasidic Wisdom: Selections Annotated & Explained* (Woodstock, VT: SkyLight Paths, 2010), 27–29.

## THREE: Avelut/Mourning

p. 40. *"All of us go down to the dust . . . Alleluia, alleluia, alleluia."*
*The Book of Common Prayer* (The Church Hymnal Corporation and The Seabury Press, 1979), 499.

pp. 40–41. *During these days, mourners are exempt . . . "border on death themselves."*
Margaret Holub, "A Cosmology of Mourning," in Debra Orenstein, ed., *Lifecycles: Jewish Women on Life Passages and Personal Milestones* (Woodstock, VT: Jewish Lights, 1994), 345–46.

pp. 41–43. *The next demarked days are shiva . . . all different pieces of commemorating, remembering, celebrating, and mourning.*
Samuel C. Heilman, *When A Jew Dies: The Ethnography of a Bereaved Son* (Berkeley: University of California Press, 2001), 119–21, 134–35, 159–60, passim.

p.41. *"they sat down with him . . . and no one spoke a word to him."*
Job 2:13 (as quoted in Heilman).

p. 43. *"'Hallowed be thy name' is . . . 'Magnified and sanctified be [God's] great name.'"*
Amy-Jill Levine, *The Misunderstood Jew: The Church and the Scandal of the Jewish Jesus* (New York: HarperOne, 2007), 45.

pp. 44–45. *Note that we hear the phrase "Come and see" . . . brought face to face with the strong reality of death.*
I owe this entire reading of "Come and See" and Jesus' weeping because he encounters death to my colleague Chuck Campbell (Professor of Homiletics at Duke Divinity School)—though I am sure I have bastardized his reading.

p. 47. *that the* Kaddish *is a curious mourner's prayer . . . the* Kaddish *is really "a Gloria."*
For the Gloria, see Heilman, 164. The most affecting recent discussion of this topic is Leon Wieseltier, *Kaddish* (New York: Knopf, 1998), 163–65.

p. 47. *"when God remembered the suffering of God's children in exile . . . causing tremors to shake the earth.."*
A summary of Berakhot 59a in L. Juliana M. Claassens, *Mourner, Mother, Midwife: Reimagining God's Delivering Presence in the Old Testament* (Louisville: Westminster John Knox Press, 2012), 24.

p. 47. *"God's love of Israel shines through his tears . . . can wreak havoc."*
Quoted in Claassens, *Mourner, Mother, Midwife*, 24.

p. 48. *Into your hands, O merciful Savior . . . the glorious company of the saints in light.* Amen.
*The Book of Common Prayer*, 499.

p. 50. *I have not said* Kaddish *. . . remember my dead.*
This list echoes Wieseltier, 173.

p. 51. *"When you mourn for your father . . . in a tradition, in a world."*
Leon Wieseltier, *Kaddish* (New York: Vintage, 2000), 556.

p. 52. *"funeral customs [that] focused on 'excessive' mourning . . . sin was the problem, not death."*
Derek Krueger, *Byzantine Christianity* (Minneapolis: Augsburg Fortress, 2010), 36.

p. 53. *"Matthew Galleli is a teacher in Rochester . . . alerts the community to the presence of a mourner."*
Katherine Ashenburg, *The Mourner's Dance: What We Do When People Die* (New York: North Point Press, 2002), 205-206.

## FOUR: Hachnassat orchim / Hospitality

p. 56. *"It is related of R. Joshua . . . 'Were you not aware that we were on our guard against you since yesterday?'"*
As quoted in Marcus van Loopik, *The Ways of the Sages and the Way of the World: The Minor Tractates of the Babylonian Talmud* (Tuebingen, Germany: Mohr Siebeck, 1991), 103.

p. 57. *"you were strangers in the land of Egypt."*
Leviticus 19:34 and Exodus 12:49.

p. 58. *"Do not be forgetful to entertain strangers; for thereby some have entertained angels unawares."*
Hebrews 13:2 KJV.

p. 58. *Rabbi Yochanan insisted that practicing hospitality . . . bowl of soup they did not like.*
"Hospitality," *Encyclopaedia Judaica*, vol. 8 (Jerusalem: Macmillan, 1971), 1030–33.
"Hospitality," *The Jewish Encyclopedia*, vol. 6 (New York: Funk and Wagnalls, 1904), 480–81.

p. 59. *"Let mutual love continue . . . entertained angels without knowing it."*
Hebrews 13:1–2.

p. 59. *"If others have plundered your property . . . For 'thereby some,' he says, 'have entertained angels unawares.'"*
From "On the Epistle to the Hebrews 33.4-5" as quoted in Erik M. Heen and Philip D. W. Krey, eds. *Hebrews* (Downers Grove, IL: InterVarsity, 2005), 305.

p .60. *In the words of one rabbi," . . . [The] world is one big hospitality inn."*
http://www.aish.com/spirituality/48ways/Way_14_Written_Instructions_For_Living.asp

p. 60. *"God offers hospitality to all humanity . . . by establishing a home . . . for all."*
Amy G. Oden, ed., *And You Welcomed Me: A Sourcebook on Hospitality in Early Christianity* (Nashville: Abingdon Press, 2001), 87, 145–214, passim.

p. 60. *"We must not look on the saints as beggars . . . and invite others to come in."*
From "Commentary on the Epistle to the Romans" as quoted in Gerald Bray, ed. *Romans* (Downers Grove, IL: InterVarsity, 1998), 305.

p. 61. *L'Arche and the Catholic Worker houses. . . .*
On practices of hospitality explicitly connected to the poor, see Christine Pohl, *Making Room: Recovering Hospitality as a Christian Tradition* (Grand Rapids, MI: Eerdmans, 1999).

p. 63. *"Visitors may be more than guests in our home. . . ."*
Karen Burton Mains, *Open Heart, Open Home: The Hospitable Way to Make Others Feel Welcome & Wanted* (Elgin, IL: David C. Cook, 1976), 21.

p. 65. *"true hospitality requires . . . receive all things from God?"*
Luke Bretherton, *Hospitality as Holiness: Christian Witness Among Moral Diversity* (Burlington, VT: Ashgate, 2006), 138.

## FIVE: Tefilla / Prayer

p. 70. *"Jews do offer freely composed prayers . . . commitment to prayer as a discipline."*
Lawrence Hoffman, *The Way into Jewish Prayer* (Woodstock, VT: Jewish Lights, 2000), 19.

p. 70. *"flexible standardization of the liturgy so that anyone attending [a] service anywhere in the country could feel at home, understand, and join in."*
http://www.americanbuddhistcongress.org/budlit.html (Accessed 2003.)

p. 71. *"A person's prayer . . . heart is in one's hands."*
As quoted in Kerry M. Olitzky, *Life's Daily Blessings: Inspiring Reflections on Gratitude and Joy for Every Day, Based on Jewish Wisdom* (Woodstock, VT: Jewish Lights, 2009), 84.

p. 72. *"Be sure to fix for yourself a place for your prayer"*
Yitzhak Buxbaum, *Jewish Spiritual Practices* (Oxford, UK: Rowman & Littlefield Publishers, 1990), 101.

p. 72. *"It is appropriate to have special clothes which you wear only for prayer."*
Buxbaum, *Jewish Spiritual Practices*, 104.

p. 74. *"May those who seek my life be disgraced . . . the angel of the LORD pursuing them."*
Psalm 35:4, 6 NIV.

p. 75. *Think that the letters of prayer . . . become one with Him.*
Quoted in *Your Word is Fire: The Hasidic Masters on Contemplative Prayer*, ed. and trans. by Arthur Green and Barry W. Holtz (Mahwah, NJ: Paulist, 1977), 42.

p. 76. *"People think that they pray to God . . . very essence of God."*
Quoted in *Your Word is Fire*, ed. and trans. by Green and Holtz, 3.

p. 77. *"If one reads the Shema and repeats it . . . until he does concentrate."*
From "Megillah 25a" elucidated by Rabbi Gedaliah Zlotowitz and Rabbi
Hersh Goldwurm in *Talmud Bavli: The Gemara, Schottenstein Edition—
Tractate Megillah*, gen. ed. Rabbi Yisroel Simcha Schorr (Brooklyn, NY:
Mesorah Publications Ltd., 1991).

pp. 78–79. *His father stopped him . . . "aleph, bet, daled, gimmel,hey, vav. . . . "*
Peninnah Schram, *The Hungry Clothes & Other Jewish Folktales* (New York:
Sterling, 2008), 66–67.

## six: Guf / Body

p. 83. *Christians, it must be admitted, have not told this story very consistently.*
A wonderful recent Christian resource on the body is Lilian Calles Barger,
*Eve's Revenge: Women and a Spirituality of the Body* (Grand Rapids, MI:
Brazos Press, 2003).

p. 85. *"Blessed are you, Hashem . . . heals all flesh and acts wondrously."*
Quoted in Judith Bendheim Guedalia, *A Neuropsychologist's Journal:
Interventions and "Judi-isms"* (Jerusalem: Urim Publications, 2012), 171.

p. 86. *Once, when Hillel . . . tomorrow it is gone.*
Quoting the Tosefta Sotah 4:13, Simkha Y. Weintraub, ed. "Some Jewish
Quotes From Over the Centuries Related to Bodily Health," *Jewish Connections
Programs*, last revised 2009, accessed February 17, 2015,
http://www.jcprograms.org/documents/BodilyHealthQuotes.pdf

p. 87. *The Talmud says . . . in honor of your Creator.*
On Shabbat 50b in Michaelson, *God in Your Body*, 137.

pp. 84–87. *"while in the bathroom it is forbidden . . ." "the taste of the Garden
of Eden in the meal."*
Yitzhak Buxbaum, *Jewish Spiritual Practices* (New York: Jason Aronson,
1994), 598, 520, 521, 277, 229, 227.

p. 87. *"creating in me many orifices . . . stand before You."*
The text of the *asher yatzar* can be found in any Orthodox Jewish prayer book,
and online at http://www.torahzone.com/AsherYatzar.htm.

p. 88. *"the Jewish girl must offset . . . the simplest clothes are the most expensive."*
Riv-Ellen Prell, *Fighting to Be Americans: Assimilation and the Trouble
Between Jewish Women and Jewish Men* (Boston: Beacon Press, 2000), 49–50.
In this paragraph, the language of "caricature" and "pathology" is drawn from

Michael Wyschogrod, The Body of Faith: God and the People of Israel (New York: The Seabury Press, 1983), 28.

p. 88. *"for rabbinic Jews, the human being was defined"* . . . . . . *"soul housed in a body."*
Daniel Boyarin, *Carnal Israel: Reading Sex in Talmudic Culture* (Berkeley: University of California Press, 1993), 5. Boyarin, in this passage and in the rest of his book, makes clear that Hellenistic Jews, like Philo, shared the Pauline perspective, privileging the dominant, normative Jewish discourse about bodies. See also Peter Brown, *The Body and Society* (New York: Columbia University Press, 1988).

p. 89. *"In regard to our bodily nature . . . a habitation of blessedness."*
From "On First Principles 3.6.6." as quoted in Gerald Bray, ed., *1-2 Corinthians* (Downers Grove, IL: InterVarsity, 1999), 169.

p. 90. *our evening bath as an opportunity to ponder and pray into the baptismal covenant.*
Stephanie Paulsell, *Honoring the Body: Meditations on a Christian Practice* (San Francisco: Jossey-Bass, 2002), 49–56.

p. 91. *"The movement of the body . . . new awareness in yourself."*
Mike Comins, *Making Prayer Real: Leading Jewish Spiritual Voices on Why Prayer is Difficult and What to Do About It* (Woodstock, VT: Jewish Lights, 2010), 67–68.

p. 92. *"When I pray, my body takes on a life of its own . . . they are trying to tell me."*
Comins, *Making Prayer Real*, 67–68.

p. 92. *Then there is the matter of suffering.*
For a helpful discussion of Christian suffering, see Paulsell, 165–80.

p. 93. *"Slowly, slowly," she writes, "MS will teach me to live as a body."*
Nancy Mairs, *Remembering the Bone House: An Erotics of Place and Space* (New York: Harper and Row, 1989), 235.

p. 93. *"Being a body is a spiritual discipline . . . living fully and gratefully as a body."*
Rowan Williams, "On Being a Human Body," *Sewanee Theological Review* 42, no. 4 (Michelmas, 1999): 413.

p. 95. *"I am going to take a bath . . . which is made in His image."*
Buxbaum, *Jewish Spiritual Practices*, 526.

p. 95. *"Or do you not know that your body is a temple . . . glorify God in your body."*
1 Corinthians 6:19–20.

p. 95. *"In the Platonic view . . . because it is in Christ."*
From "On the Soul 54.5" as quoted in Bray, ed., *1-2 Corinthians*, 56.

pp. 96–97. *"In Paul's letters . . . threw dramatic shadows."*
Peter Brown, *The Body and Society: Men, Women, and Sexual Renunciation in Early Christianity* (New York: Columbia University Press, 1988), 47.

p. 98. *"The translator's shift . . . What else do we know in the body?"*
Jennifer A. Glancy, *Corporal Knowledge: Early Christian Bodies* (New York: Oxford University Press, 2010), 3.

## SEVEN: Tzum/Fasting

p. 104. *Once two brothers . . . fulfill the commandment to refresh others.*
Quoted in Joan Chittister, *Illuminated Life: Monastic Wisdom for Seekers of Light* (Maryknoll, NY: Orbis, 2000), 100.

p. 104. *A brother said to an old man . . . the "new commandment" to love one another.*
Quoted in Andrew Harvey ed., *The Essential Mystics: The Soul's Journey into Truth* (New York: Castle Books, 1998), 185.

p. 104. *A leader of a community asked Abba Poemen . . . to the fear of God.*
Benedicta Ward, trans. *The Sayings of the Desert Fathers: The Alphabetical Collection* (Collegeville, MD: Liturgical Press, 1984), 161.

p. 105. *And the Gospel of Matthew makes this scary, flat claim: there are demons that "go not out but by prayer and fasting."*
Matthew 17:21. Scholars believe this verse is not part of the original Gospel text. You can find it in the footnotes of most annotated study Bibles. It will also be found in the KJV, ASN, and NASB.

p. 106. *As journalist Christine Gardner . . . 43,000 member churches.*
Christine J. Gardner, "Hungry for God: Why More and More Christians Are Fasting for Revival," *Christianity Today* (April 5, 1999), 32.

p. 107. *"The whole rationale of symbolic gestures . . . the observance of fasting and abstinence."*
Eamon Duffy, "To Fast Again," *First Things*, no. 151 (2005): 4–6.

p. 107. *In* A Closer Walk, *she describes. . . .*
Catherine Marshall, *A Closer Walk*, excerpted in Richard J. Foster and Emilie Griffin, eds., *Spiritual Classics* (San Francisco: HarperSanFrancisco, 2002), 57–59.

p. 108. *"Master of the Worlds . . . and may You show me favor."*
From "Berachos 17a" elucidated by Rabbi Dealiah Zlotowitz in *Talmud Bavli: The Gemara, Schottenstein Daf Yomi Edition—Tractate Berachos,* gen. eds. Rabbi Yisroel Simcha Schorr, Rabbi Chaim Malinowitz, and R' Hersh Goldwurm, Vol. I (Brooklyn, NY: Mesorah, 1997).

p. 109. *"a perfect quieting of all our impulses, fleshly and spiritual."*
St. Thomas Aquinas quoted in E. E. Holmes, *Prayer and Practice, or, "Three Noble Duties"* (London: Longmans, Green, 1911), 110.

p. 110. *"Take heed that you do nor make fasting . . . Forgive them their trespasses."*
From "Homily 1, On Fasting" as quoted in Thomas C. Oden and Christopher A. Hall, eds. *Mark* (Downers Grove, IL: InterVarsity, 1998), 31.

p. 111. *I was lecturing . . . But, it was a beginning.*
Amy Laura Hall, "On Eating Chocolate for Lent," *J. Kameron Carter* [Blog], March 9, 2011, http://jkameroncarter.com/?p=1003, accessed February 19, 2015.

pp. 112–113. *"Sacramental fasting does not posit . . . chooses to gift us with divine life."*
Joyce Ann Zimmerman, "Fasting as Feasting," *Liturgical Ministry* 19, no. 2 (2010): 76–77.

pp. 114–115. *For David, as for everyone in the Bible . . . afflicting one's spirit and one's self."*
Scot McKnight, *Fasting: The Ancient Practices* (Nashville: Thomas Nelson, 2009), xv.

p. 117. *"people to their bodies, to their communities, and to their most sacred values."*
Michelle Lelwica, *The Religion of Thinness: Satisfying the Spiritual Hungers Behind Women's Obsession with Food and Weight* (Carlsbad, CA: Gürze Books, 2010), 151.

## EIGHT: Hiddur p'nai zaken / Aging

p. 119. *Once upon a time, the midrash says, . . . age spots and gray whiskers.*
Dayle A. Friedman, "Crown Me With Wrinkles and Gray Hair: Examining Traditional Jewish Views of Aging." In Susan Berrin, ed., *A Heart of Wisdom: Making the Jewish Journey From Midlife Through the Elder Years* (Woodstock, VT: Jewish Lights, 1997), p.5. Genesis Rabbah 65:9.

p. 119. *The young are not to contradict anything their elders say . . . in case an older person should enter the room.*
Friedman, 11.

p. 119. *A contemporary Jewish poet, Danny Siegel, has also offered a creative reading of the biblical injunctions about the elderly. . . .*
Danny Siegel, "The Mitzvah of Bringing Out the Beauty of Our Elders' Faces," in Berrin, 50–52. *Hiddur p'nai zaken*, the idea of honoring the face of one's elder, derives from Leviticus 19:32. I take my inspiration for the title of this chapter from Danny Siegel.

p.120. *"I don't ever want to be . . . spending time with her."*
Letty Cottin Pogrebin, *Getting Over Getting Older* (New York: Time Warner, 1996), 304–5.

pp. 122–123. *Put it firmly in your mind . . . It's life-giving and life-long.*
"Prayers, Litanies and Words of Wisdom on Growing Older," *Committee on Aging, the Episcopal Diocese of Maryland,* last revised 1999, accessed February 17, 2015, http://tinyurl.com/os5avry

p. 124. *He speaks instead of "eldering." . . . or, in another of Reb Zalman's clever infinitives, "to sage."*
Zalman Schacter-Shalomi, *From Age-ing to Sage-ing: A Profound New Vision of Growing Older* (New York: Warner Books, 1997).

p. 124. *The Hebrew word* sayvah *. . . the process of setting wrong things right.*
Susan Berrin, ed., *A Heart of Wisdom: Making the Jewish Journey from Mid-Life Through the Elder Years* (Woodstock, VT: Jewish Lights Publishing, 1999) 33–34.

p. 125. *"women were relegated . . . her sins and transgressions."*
Connie L. Scarborough, *"Celestina*: The Power of Old Age," in *Old Age in the Middle Ages and the Renaissance: Interdisciplinary Approaches to a Neglected Topic,* ed. Albrecht Classen (Berlin, Germany: Walter de Gruyter, 2007), 344–345.

p. 126. *In the Middle Ages. . . . It is also about prayer and attention and preparation and God.*
Shulamith Shahar, *Growing Old in the Middle Ages,* trans. Yael Lotan (New York: Routledge, 1997), 54–59.

p. 126. *It is worth noting that through the nineteenth century. . . .*
For a history of American attitudes toward death, see Gary Laderman, *The Sacred Remains: American Attitudes Toward Death, 1799–1883* (New Haven: Yale University Press, 1999).

p. 127. *"Just as sin entered the world . . . justification that brings life for all men."*
Romans 5:12, 18 NIV.

p. 127. *Letty Cottin Pogrebin titles one chapter. . . .*
Pogrebin, 299.

p. 128. *"It is of course a fact . . . old and young alike."*
Rowan Williams, "Archbishop – older People 'are still participants in society, not passengers,'" Full Text of Opening Speech, last updated December 14, 2012, accessed February 17, 2015, http://tinyurl.com/ncbgqhl

p. 129. *they "participat[ed] . . . in an active social life and enjoy[ed] a culture built out of a cherished common past."*
Barbara Myerhoff, *Number Our Days* (New York: E. P. Dutton, 1978), 217–18.

p. 130. *As Kathleen Fischer has explained . . ."Our stories then take on . . . meaning as a part of a larger story that redeems and embraces them."*
Kathleen Fischer, *Winter Grace: Spirituality and Aging* (Nashville: Upper Room Books, 1998) 48–49.

p. 131. *"moves more slowly now . . . our own aging selves."*
Moers Wenig, "God Is a Woman, and She Is Growing Older," in Rifat Sonsio, *The Many Faces of God: A Reader of Modern Jewish Theologies* (New York: URJ, 2004), 241–48.

p. 132. *Contemporary America has done a pretty good job . . . the day you buy a wheelchair.*
Barbara Myerhoff, *Remembered Lives: The Work of Ritual, Storytelling, and Growing Older* (Ann Arbor: The University of Michigan Press, 1972).

p. 133. *"Until Abraham there was no old age . . . 'the hoary head is a crown of glory.'"*
"Genesis Rabbah 65:9", as quoted in Abigail Treu, "Between the Lines—Hayyei Sarah," *The Jewish Theological Seminary*, Weekly Midrash Learning, accessed February 17, 2015, http://tinyurl.com/o4ghqsb

pp. 134–135. *Let everyone above all have this zeal . . . we receive it back imperishable.*
From "Life of St. Anthony 16.3-8" as quoted in Quentin F. Wesselschmidt, ed. *Psalms 51-150* (Downers Grove, IL: InterVarsity, 2007), 168.

## NINE: Hadlakat nerot/Candle-lighting

p. 137. *"Candles [are] everywhere"* . . . *"and I mean* everywhere.*"*
Ana Veciana Suarez, "Waxing Poetic: Electric Light Doesn't Cut It," *Miami Herald*, December 22, 2002.

p. 137. *"It is difficult to imagine a more primal ritual . . . yearning [for] its source on high."*
Lawrence Kushner and Nehemia Polen, *Filling Words with Light: Hasidic and Mystical Reflections on Jewish Prayer* (Woodstock, VT: Jewish Lights, 2004), 127.

p. 138. *"As a ceremonial object or art . . . allow them to 'illumine our eyes.'"*
Siegal, Strassfeld, and Sharon, *The First Jewish Catalog*, 42.

p. 139. *"Always light a special candle . . . "'with lights, glorify God.'"*
Buxbaum, *Jewish Spiritual Practices*, 102.

p. 139. *Candlemaking as we know it . . . the twelfth century.*
"Candles," *Encyclopaedia Judaica*, vol. 5 (Jerusalem: Macmillan, 1971), 117–19.

p. 140. *"On Shabbat, the observant Jew . . . absorb the light."*
Brenda Miller, *Season of the Body: Essays*, as quoted in Cait Johnson, *Earth, Water, Fire, and Air: Essential Ways of Connecting to the Spirit* (Woodstock, VT: SkyLight Paths, 2003), 133.

p. 140. *After you light the candles, you close your eyes and beckon. . . .*
See Nina Beth Cardin, *The Tapestry of Jewish Time: A Spiritual Guide to Holidays and Life-Cycle Events* (Springfield, NJ: Behrman House, 2000), 39. Cardin explains another reason for covering the eyes before saying the blessing over the candles: "By reciting a blessing before we enjoy the goodness in our lives, we can enhance the experience and sharpen our appreciation of it. For example we recite the blessing over bread before we eat. However, because Shabbat begins when we say the blessing over the candles and it is forbidden to kindle a fire on Shabbat, we light the candles first and then recite the blessing, covering our eyes so that we do not enjoy the Sabbath light until after we have completed the blessing."

p. 140. *Adam was frightened at the end of the first Shabbat. . . .*
Midrash Rabbah 11:2.

p. 141. *"All the darkness . . . illuminate all the darkness."*
Quoted in Maxine Rose Schur, *Hannah Szenes: A Song of Light* (Philadelphia: The Jewish Publication Society, 1985), 58.

p. 143. *"Blessed is the match . . . consumed in kindling flame."*
Quoted in Hannah Senesh and Eitan Senesh, *Hannah Senesh: Her Life and Diary, The First Complete Edition* (Woodstock, VT: Jewish Lights, 2004), 306.

p. 142. *There is a story in the Talmud about Rabbi Jose. . . . "we can see clearly from one end of [the] world to the other."*
Michael Strassfeld, *A Book of Life: Embracing Judaism as a Spiritual Practice* (New York: Schocken Books, 2002), 288.

p. 143. *"Think of a dark time in your own life . . . leave the darkness behind?"*
Penina V. Adelman, *Miriam's Well: Rituals for Jewish Women Around the Year*, 2nd ed. (New York: Biblio, 1990), 39.

p. 144. *"The aura of a candle . . . reaching for that presence."*
Zalman Schachter-Shalomi and Joel Segel, *Jewish With Feeling: A Guide to Meaningful Jewish Practice* (New York: Riverhead, 2005), 51.

p. 144. *Candles have failed to cross the gender gap. They're a chick thing.*
Suarez, "Waxing Poetic."

pp. 144–45. *There is an old Jewish folk custom called "the laying of wicks" . . . "rectify the sin by which they brought death to the world."*
Chava Weissler, *Voices of the Matriarchs: Listening to the Prayers of Early Modern Jewish Women* (Boston: Beacon Press, 1999), 133–44.

p. 146. *"Afterwards, this holy person . . . by him to everlasting bliss."*
*The Life of Blessed Henry Suso by Himself*, trans. Thomas Francis Knox (London: Burns, Lambert, and Oates, 1865), Chapter XLIX, accessed March 23, 2015, http://www.ccel.org/ccel/suso/susolife

p. 147. *The day is o'er . . . Cause all gloom to vanish.*
Frances Elizabeth Cox, trans. *Hymns from the Germans*, 2nd ed. (London: 1864), accessed February 17, 2015, http://www.gutenberg.org/files/39439/39439-h/39439-h.htm.

p. 148. *Poet and teacher Yiskah Rosenfeld has written . . . "our over-committed schedules."*
Yiskah Rosenfeld, "Taking Back Our Rites: Lighting Candles, Baking Challah, and the Laws of Married Sex," Lilith 26, no. 2 (2001): 22.

pp. 148–149. *"You shall further command the Israelites . . . throughout their generations by the Israelites."*
Exodus 27:20–21.

pp. 150–151. *"As he himself will explain a little later . . . worthy to receive the divine light."*
From "Commentary on the Apocalypse" as quoted in William C. Weinrich, ed. *Revelation* (Downers Grove, IL: InterVarsity, 2005), 11. Revelation 1:20.

pp. 151–152. *"reads more like an affirmation of faith . . . a renewed sense of optimism and purpose.'"*
Olitzky, *Life's Daily Blessings*, 22–23.

## TEN:  Kiddushin / Weddings

p. 155. *It is only with Jesus' stern words to the Pharisees. . . .*
For an accessible, cogent discussion of the New Testament on divorce, see Richard Hays, *The Moral Vision of the New Testament: A Contemporary Introduction to New Testament Ethics* (San Francisco: HarperSanFrancisco, 1996), 347–78.

p. 157. *"bone of my bones and flesh of my flesh."*
Genesis 2:23 NIV.

p. 159. *"According to the will of the one who gave the command . . . abundantly for the couple's future."*
From "Commentary on John 1.2.6-7" as quoted in Joel C. Elowsky, ed. *Ancient Christian Commentary on Scripture: John 1-10* (Downers Grove, IL: InterVarsity, 2006), 97.

p. 161. *"How many mysteries are hidden . . . the nails of His crucifixion."*
"Syrian Wedding Liturgy," as quoted in Sam Torode and Bethany Torode, comps. *Aflame: Ancient Wisdom on Marriage* (Grand Rapids, MI: Eerdmans, 2005), 37.

p. 162. *"Bestow abundant joy . . . rejoice with his bride."*
From "The Tractate Ketubot 7b-8a," as quoted in Ben Zion Bokser, trans., ed. and Baruch M. Bokser, ed. *The Talmud: Selected Writings* (Mahwah, NJ: Paulist, 1989), 141–142.

pp. 164–167. *Everyone else at the banquet . . . let him know you got the point.*
Barbara Brown Taylor, "Exposed! The Imposter Syndrome." Sermon, Duke University Chapel, Durham, NC, October 12, 2008. Video accessed February 17, 2015, http://tinyurl.com/n9q5ut4

## ELEVEN: Mezuzot/Doorposts

p. 168. *"You shall love the* LORD. *. . your house and on your gates."*
Deuteronomy 6:5, 6, 9 NASB.

p. 169. *Historian Colleen McDannell, for example . . . helped sanctify the home.*
Colleen McDannell, *The Christian Home in Victorian America 1840-1900* (Bloomington: Indiana University Press, 1994), 83, 39.

p. 170. *Jews got serious . . . slices of parchment.*
Erika Meitner, "The *Mezuzah*: American Judaism and Constructions of American Sacred Space," unpublished paper in author's possession, 6.

pp. 171–172. *"and affixes a mezuzah to his door . . . protect him from sinning."*
Talmud, Masechet Menahot, 43b.
*Mezuzot* are connected to protection in another way as well. They recall the story of the Exodus from Egypt, in which the Israelites marked their doors with slashes of blood. When the Angel of Death came to slay the firstborn of every Egyptian family, the Israelites—identified, and protected, by their sanguinary doorpost markings—were spared.

p. 173. *The doorpost played an important part . . . "He will not suffer the destroyer to come in unto your houses"*
Abraham P. Bloch, *The Biblical and Historical Background of Jewish Customs and Ceremonies* (Jersey City, NJ: KTAV, 1980), 83.

p. 172. *Perhaps the most startling Charlottesville mezuzah . . . "you don't have to hide it."*
Meitner, 12.

pp. 177–178. *I walk my new husband, Jim . . . forgiving, creative, and passionate.*
Marian Nash, "Pausing at the Doorpost," *Lilith* 36, no. 1 (2011): 36–37.

# GLOSSARY OF
# Hebrew and Yiddish Terms

(Terms are Hebrew unless marked as Yiddish.)

*Amidah*: Central prayer of Jewish services, composed in the fifth century CE.

*aninut*: State of mourning between death and burial.

*asher yatzar*: Literally, "who formed"; blessing recited every morning and after one has gone to the bathroom; expresses recognition that bodies are complex and sophisticated systems.

*Av*: The fifth month in the Jewish calendar. (The ninth of Av is a fast day that commemorates the destruction of the Temple.)

*avelut*: Entire period of mourning.

*bat mitzvah*: "Daughter of the commandments"; girl who has reached the age of twelve and becomes obligated to observe all the commandments.

*brit milah* (often shortened to *bris* or *brit*): Circumcision ceremony at which an eight-day-old boy enters the covenant of Abraham.

*challah*: Egg bread, often braided, that is traditionally eaten on the Sabbath.

*cholent*: Stew consisting of meat, potatoes, and beans simmered overnight; typically served on the Sabbath.

*chuppah* (pl. *chuppot*): Wedding canopy.

*fleishig* (Yiddish): Consisting of, prepared with, or relating to meat or meat products.

*guf*: Body.

*hachnassat orchim*: The welcoming of guests.

*hadlakat nerot*: Lighting candles.

*Hasidic*: Relating to Hasidism, a form of mystical Orthodox Judaism that began in the 1700s in Eastern Europe.

*havdalah*: Literally, "separation"; the ceremony that concludes the Sabbath.

*Kaddish*: An Aramaic prayer, central to Jewish liturgy, that praises and glorifies God. The "Mourner's Kaddish" is an iteration of the prayer said by those in mourning. Many commentators have pointed out and, indeed, puzzled over the fact that the Mourner's Kaddish does not mention mourning or bereavment, per se. Some of these commentators have suggested that the work of the prayer is not, strictly speaking, to commemorate the dead, but to point the mourner's attention toward God.

*kashrut*: Jewish dietary laws.

*kavannah*: Intention that allows one to offer words or deeds as gifts of inner devotion.

*ketubah*: Marriage contract.

*kiddush*: Literally, "sanctification"; a benediction sung or recited over a cup of wine to consecrate the Sabbath or a festival.

*kiddushin*: Literally, "sanctity" or "setting apart"; also used as a synonym for marriage.

*Kol asher diber Adonai na'aseh ve-nishma*: "All the words that God has spoken, we will do and we will hear"; from Exodus 24.

*mezuzah* (pl. *mezuzot*): Literally, "doorpost"; small piece of parchment inscribed with the biblical passages Deuteronomy 6:4–9 and 11:13–21. The parchment is rolled up in a container and affixed to a door frame. *Mezuzah* also denotes the container that holds the parchment.

*midrash*: Literally, "investigation"; stories elaborating on incidents in the Bible to derive a principle of Jewish law or provide a moral lesson.

*mikvah*: Pool used for purposes of ritual purification.

*Mishnah*: Collection of rulings and laws under the leadership of Rabbi Judah Hanasi, collected about 210 CE. These had been passed on orally for a number of generations.

*mitzvah* (pl. *mitzvot*): Commandment; two types are *mitzvot asei* (positive commandments: "Thou shalt") and *mitzvot lo ta'aseh* (prohibitions: "Thou shalt not").

*ner tamid*: Eternal light; continually burning lamp that was to be placed in the Tent of Meeting and later in the Temple. Found in contemporary synagogues in front of the cabinet that holds the Torah scrolls.

*neshamah yeteirah*: Literally, "additional soul"; said to embody the height of spiritual happiness created by the Sabbath.
*olam haba*: The world to come.

*Rosh Hashanah*: Jewish new year.

*seudat havra'ah*: Meal of condolence served to mourners on their return from the funeral.

*Shabbat*: Seventh day of the week; a day of rest.

*Shabbat haMalkah:* Literally, the Sabbath queen; image of the Sabbath as a queen to be honored and welcomed.

*shalom bayit*: Peace in the home; harmony between family members.

*shechitah*: Ritual slaughter of animals that may be eaten in accordance with Jewish law.

*Shema*: Prayer consisting of verses from Deuteronomy 6:4–9, 11:13–21, and Numbers 15:37–41.

*sheva brachot*: Seven blessings recited at a Jewish wedding.

*shin*: שׁ, A letter of the Hebrew alphabet.

*shiva*: Seven days of mourning following a person's burial.

*shloshim*: Literally, "thirty"; thirty-day mourning period following a person's burial.

*shofar*: Ram's horn.

*shul* (Yiddish): Synagogue.

*Shulchan Aruch*: Literally, "a set table"; the code of laws and practices published in 1567 by Joseph Caro of the Galilee (1488–1575), with additions by Moses Isserles of Cracow (1520–70).

*siddur*: Prayer book.

*Talmud*: Literally, "teaching"; usually refers to the Babylonian Talmud, completed about 500 CE, a collection of the discussions and decisions of the Rabbis from about 300 to 500 CE. These discussions were an elaboration and clarification of the laws of the *Mishnah*.

*tefillah*: Prayer.

*teshuva*: Repentance.

*Torah*: Handwritten scroll of the Five Books of Moses.

*tzitzit*: Fringes.

*tzom*: Fast or fasting.

*tzom shtikah:* A fast of silence; medieval kabbalistic practice in which one refrains from speaking.

*yahrtzeit* (Yiddish): Anniversary of a person's death on the Jewish calendar.

*yichud*: Literally, "privacy" or "union"; term for the private time between the bride and groom that constitutes the final stage of the marriage ceremony.

*Yom Kippur*: Day of Atonement.

# ABOUT PARACLETE PRESS

# Also available from Paraclete Press . . .

## Mudhouse Sabbath
The Workshop DVD
Lauren F. Winner

ISBN: 978-1-55725-683-6, $29.95, 65 minutes

Through the expertise and personal experiences of Lauren Winner, this DVD will challenge you to practice your faith in ways that are biblical, Christlike, and imminently practical.

## Midrash: Reading the Bible with Question Marks
Rabbi Sandy Eisenberg Sasso

ISBN: 978-1-61261-416-8, $14.99, Paperback

Rabbi Sasso explores how Midrash originated, how it is still used today, and offers new translations and interpretations of more than twenty essential Midrash texts.

## Let Us Break Bread Together
A Passover Haggadah for Christians
Pastor Michael A. Smith and Rabbi Rami Shapiro

ISBN: 978-1-55725-444-3, $15.99, French-flap paperback

There are many haggadot used in Jewish homes and synagogues, but this one offers meaningful insights on how Christians can both learn from Judaism as a means of deepening their Christian faith, and better understand the Jewishness of Jesus.